SPEAK BUSINESS
ENGLISH
LIKE AN AMERICAN

LEARN THE IDIOMS & EXPRESSIONS
YOU NEED TO SUCCEED ON THE JOB!

DELUXE BOOK & CD SET

AMY GILLETT

Worldwide sale ex Taiwan & Hong Kong
authorized by Language Success Press

Originally published by Language Success Press
This annotated English–Chinese bilingual edition published under special
agreement with the proprietor for sale in Taiwan and Hong Kong only.

Published by Bookman Books, Ltd. 2006
3F, 60, Roosevelt Road Section 4, Taipei 100, Taiwan
Printed in Taiwan

定　　價／300元
出 版 者／書林出版有限公司
　　　　　100台北市羅斯福路四段60號三樓
　　　　　Tel: 02-23684938・23687226　Fax: 02-66329771
　　　　　http://www.bookman.com.tw
經銷事業／Tel: 02-23684938#103・119　Fax: 02-66329770
學校業務／02-23687226・04-23763799・07-2290300
發 行 人／蘇正隆
郵　　撥／15743873・書林出版有限公司
登 記 證／局版臺業字第一八三一號
出版日期／2006年5月一版
ISBN 957-445-137-2

bells and whistles the name of the game track record the best of both worlds on top of trends through the roof on the same page nothing

TABLE OF CONTENTS

pull out all the stops a pat on the back cash cow step up to the plate dream up on the right track generate lots of buzz more bank for the buck wear many hats

bells and whistles the name of the game track record the best of both worlds on top of t̶ nothing is set in stone put a stake i̶ a nutshell nothing to sneeze at a pat on the back cash cow step up to the plate dream up on

INTRODUCTION

For better or worse, the American workplace is full of idioms. People don't begin a project. They **get a project off the ground**. They don't call each other to discuss progress. They **touch base**. Later, if the project is not going well, they don't end it. They **pull the plug**.

不管是好是壞，美國職場充滿了各種片語。他們不說「開始」一項案件，而是說讓「案件破土」；不說「打電話討論」，而是說來「觸壘」；如果稍後案子進行順利，也不說「結束」專案，而是「拔掉插頭」。

Speak Business English Like An American covers over 350 idioms and expressions you're likely to encounter in today's business world. Familiarize yourself with all of them. When they come up in conversation, you'll be prepared to respond confidently instead of becoming silent while thinking to yourself, "What's he talking about? Sales went **through the roof**? What roof?" As you're asking yourself these questions, the conversation is continuing without you. Suddenly you're left behind. Before you know it, you're **out of the loop**.

本書包含超過350個職場常用的片語，請好好學習熟悉這些片語，這樣一來如果對話中出現了這些片語，你會胸有成竹，而不是沉默以對，偷偷想著：「他在說什麼啊？銷售『長紅』？多長多紅？」當你在納悶的時候，別人早就不知道說到哪裡去了，而你被晾在一旁。等到你會意的時候，你早就「出局」了。

After getting to know the idioms, listen for them in everyday conversations and look for them in newspapers. Idioms are everywhere. Newspapers like the *Wall Street Journal* and business sections of daily newspapers are full of these idioms. Once you get a good feel for them, try them out on your colleagues and friends. Idioms will add color and excitement to your language. Using idioms will make you sound more like a native speaker.

了解這些片語之後，試著在每日的生活會話中、報紙上搜尋這些片語的蹤跡。片語俯拾即是，例如《華爾街日報》和某些報紙的財經版都常出現。等你熟悉這些片語，就可以和同事朋友講這些片語。片語可以為語言增色，使用片語讓你的英文說得更道地。

Let's take just one example. Let's say you're losing a lot of business to your competition. You could say, "We're losing business to our competition." Or, you could say, "Our competition is **eating our lunch!**" The second sentence sounds a little more lively, doesn't it?

　　舉個例子吧。你快輸給某個競爭對手一筆生意，你可以說：「我們快輸給對手一筆生意。」也可以說：「對手正在吃掉我們的大餅！」第二種說法聽起來是不是更生動？

Don't feel the need to load every sentence with idioms. A well-placed idiom here and there will **do the trick**.

　　別認為每句話都應塞進幾個片語，恰到好處地點綴一個片語即可「奏效」。

You don't have to add every idiom in this book to your active vocabulary. You'll naturally find some more useful than others. A few of the idioms in this book — such as **think outside the box** and **on the same page** — have become so common, they're now overused. But even if you don't want to use them, you should understand them since you're likely to hear them.

　　書中教的片語不用每個都拿來應用，你自然會發現某些片語比較有用。有些片語像「思考跳脫窠臼」、「觀念一致」就很普遍，幾乎被濫用了。但即便你不想使用這些片語，你仍應了解它們，因為你會常常聽到這些片語。

American English idioms come from many different sources. The business-focused idioms often originate from military speak (example: **rally the troops**) and from the world of sports (example: **step up to the plate**). This provides some insight into the way Americans think about business: like war, it's a bitter competition with winners and losers. Like sports, it's a game, with the prizes going to those teams (companies) with superior strategy and execution.

美式英語的片語來自許多典故。通常商業方面的片語源自軍隊用語（例如 rally the troops）和運動用語（例如step up the plate）。由此我們可以發現美國人是如何看待商業行為：商場如戰場，競爭激烈，有贏家和輸家；商業活動也是種運動、遊戲，策略與執行力優越的團隊就可得獎。

For your convenience, all of the idioms in this book are shown in bold and listed in the *Index*. In the *Glossary of Terms*, we've included definitions for many other words and phrases that you may not understand. These terms are in italics in the dialogues. Whenever you see an italicized word you don't know, just turn to the back of the book to look it up.

為了方便學習，本書所有的片語都以粗體標示，並列入索引。對話裡有一些字你可能不懂，都以斜體標示，並收進詞彙表中。遇到不會的斜體字，可以翻到書末查詢。

This book comes with a CD featuring all of the dialogues. The CD will help you master the rhythm and stress of American English speech. It will also help you remember the idioms. Play it at home, at work, in the car, while on business trips...before you know it, you'll be speaking English like a native!

本書附有一片CD，包含所有對話。CD可以幫你熟習美式英語的韻律和重音，有助於記憶和背誦。你可以在家聽、工作聽、車上聽、出差時聽，這樣一來你很快就可以說出一口道地的英語！

Good luck adding idioms to your everyday speech. It's fun and it'll help you succeed in the working world!

祝你好運！好好運用剛學到的片語，用片語說英語不僅好玩，還可以讓你在職場上無往不利！

SPEAK
BUSINESS
ENGLISH
LIKE AN
AMERICAN

TALKING ABOUT A NEW PROJECT
為新產品提出構想

Carl, Greg, and Anne work for WaterSonic Corporation. Recently, the company has come up with an idea for a new electric toothbrush.

Carl: I think we've **come up with a winner**.

Anne: I agree. The new Brush-o-matic toothbrush should be a **blockbuster**!

Carl: Our designers have already made up some *prototypes*.*
The toothbrushes have a tooth-whitening attachment and many other **bells and whistles**.

Greg: We should **fast track this project**. Let's try to *launch* it in time for the holiday season.

Anne: This will be a great **stocking stuffer**!

Carl: We definitely need a **big win** for the holidays.

Anne: This is a great idea. We're going to **make a killing**.

Greg: Let's not talk about this project to anybody who doesn't need to know. We'll **keep it under wraps**.

Carl: I agree. **Mum's the word**. We don't want any of our competitors to **get wind of** the idea and **rip it off**!

Anne: Right. Let's meet again on Monday morning and discuss our **game plan** for **getting this project off the ground**!

* 本書斜體單字片語之中譯與英解，請參閱 P.187-191。

IDIOMS & EXPRESSIONS - LESSON 1

(to) come up with a winner 提出絕佳構想
to think up a very good idea

EXAMPLE: Everybody likes Pepsi's new advertising campaign. Their advertising agency has **come up with a winner**.

. . . .

blockbuster 大熱門／暢銷品／熱賣
a big success; a huge hit

EXAMPLE: Eli Lilly made a lot of money with the prescription drug, Prozac. It was a real **blockbuster**.

ORIGIN: This term comes from the blockbuster bombs used during World War Two by the British Royal Air Force. They were huge and created a large explosive force. Blockbuster ideas similarly create a big impact — and hopefully don't cause destruction like blockbuster bombs!

. . . .

bells and whistles 附加功能
extra product features, usually using the latest technologies; product features which are attractive, but not essential for the product to function

EXAMPLE: Our office just got a new copier with all the **bells and whistles**. I'll probably never learn how to use all of its features!

. . . .

(to) fast track a project 加速進行一項專案
to make a project a high priority; to speed up the time frame of a project

EXAMPLE: Let's **fast track this project**. We've heard rumors that our competitors are developing similar products.

. . . .

stocking stuffer 耶誕禮物
a small gift given at Christmas time

EXAMPLE: These new mini travel pillows will make great **stocking stuffers**!

NOTE: This expression comes from the practice of kids hanging up stockings that Santa Claus fills (or "stuffs") with small gifts.

big win 明星商品／暢銷單品
a huge success; a successful product

EXAMPLE: The drug company spent millions on research and development, hoping that one of their new products would be a **big win**.

.....

(to) make a killing 大撈一筆／大賺一筆
to make a lot of money

EXAMPLE: Suzanne **made a killing** on her Google stock and retired at 40.

SYNONYM: to make a fortune

.....

(to) keep something under wraps 保密／對外不漏口風
to keep something secret; to not let anybody know about a new project or plan

EXAMPLE: I'm sorry I can't tell you anything about the project I'm working on. My boss told me to **keep it under wraps**.

NOTE: "Wraps" are things that provide cover, so if something is "under wraps" it's covered up and hidden.

.....

mum's the word 閉口不談
let's keep quiet about this; I agree not to tell anyone about this

EXAMPLE: Please don't tell anybody about our new project. Remember: **mum's the word**!

ORIGIN: The word "mum" comes from the murmur "mmmmm," the only sound you can make when your mouth is shut firmly. Try making other sounds besides "mmmmm" with your lips and mouth shut firmly, and you will see that it's impossible!

.....

(to) get wind of 發現／得知
to find out about something, often sensitive information

EXAMPLE: When the restaurant owner **got wind of** the fact that one of his waiters was stealing money from the cash register, he was furious.

(to) rip off   竊取／盜用他人構想
to copy an idea; to steal

EXAMPLE: Why doesn't the Donox Company ever think up any original ideas? All they ever do is **rip off** their competitors!

NOTE: "Rip off" is also a noun. Example: We were charged $10,000 for a small advertisement in the newspaper. What a **rip off**!

game plan   策略／計劃
an action plan; a plan for how a project will proceed

EXAMPLE: The software company's **game plan** is to expand its operations into China and India over the next year.

ORIGIN: In football, a "game plan" is a strategy for winning.

(to) get something off the ground   付諸行動／實行
to get started on something, often a project

EXAMPLE: We've been sitting around talking about this project for months. It's time to take action and **get it off the ground**!

✎ PRACTICE THE IDIOMS

Choose the best substitute for the phrase or sentence in bold:

1) Did the company think of this new product idea themselves? **No, they ripped it off from an inventor.**
   a) No, they paid an inventor for the idea.
   b) No, they stole the idea from an inventor.
   c) No, they discussed it with an inventor and he agreed to sell it to them.

2) Andrea is planning to quit her job at the end of September, but **mum's the word**.
   a) don't tell anybody
   b) don't tell her mother
   c) she may change her mind

6

3) Sony has **made a killing on** its popular PlayStation line.
   a) lost money on
   b) made a lot of money on
   c) decided to stop producing

4) After receiving a large loan from the bank, the company was finally able to **get its project off the ground**.
   a) get started on the project
   b) cancel the project
   c) borrow money

5) That new software company seems very disorganized. Do they have a **game plan**?
   a) a plan for closing down their business
   b) a plan for developing new games
   c) a plan for how they will proceed to grow their business

6) Some experts recommend that when you're interviewing for a new job, you **keep your current salary under wraps**.
   a) you should tell the interviewer what your current salary is
   b) you should say you're making twice as much as you're   really earning
   c) you should not say how much you're currently earning

7) Don's new cell phone has a video camera and all sorts of other **bells and whistles**.
   a) fancy features
   b) things that make loud ringing noises and whistle tones
   c) features typical in a low-priced product

8) When investors **got wind of** the fact that the pharmaceutical company's major drug increased the risk of heart attacks, the company's stock price fell.
   a) hid
   b) discovered
   c) got fed up over

ANSWERS TO LESSON 1, p. 199

I did some back-of-the-envelope calculations.

TALKING ABOUT FINANCIAL ISSUES
談論新產品線的財務及成本分析

Juan and Diane work in the finance department of Delicious Delights, a company that makes snack foods. Here, they're discussing the financial projections for a new product line.

Juan: I'm really excited about the *launch* of our new line of fat-free Delicious Delight donuts.

Diane: Me too. But before we go any further, we'd better make sure this *product line* is going to be profitable.

Juan: I did some **back-of-the-envelope calculations**. Take a look.

Diane: I see you've estimated $2 million for the new equipment. Where did you get that *figure?*

Juan: That's an **educated guess** based on some equipment I bought last year.

Diane: You're going to need to *double-check* that. Using old estimates can get us **in hot water**.

Juan: No problem. I'll get on the phone with the manufacturer in Dallas and get a *price quote*.

Diane: Do you have a sense for *market demand?* We should get the *forecasts* from the marketing department before we **crunch the numbers**.

Juan: We don't have those yet. Mary from marketing said maybe we'd have them next week.

Diane: It just **blows my mind** when marketing people want us to **run numbers**, and they don't bring us the information we need!

Juan: If we end up **in the red** on this project, it's going to be their **heads on the chopping block**, not ours. They're the ones with P&L* responsibility!

Diane: Our CFO* won't **give this project the green light** until he sees all the numbers. If it doesn't look like we'll make money or at least **break even**, he'll **pull the plug** on the project.

*P&L – profit & loss. Those with P&L responsibility are in charge of making sure the business makes a profit. They manage the "P&L statement," also called the "income statement." This shows the financial results of operations over a certain time period, usually a month, a quarter, or a year.

* CFO – chief financial officer. The senior manager responsible for the financial activities of a company.

IDIOMS & EXPRESSIONS - LESSON 2

back-of-the-envelope calculations 粗略的估算
quick calculations; estimates using approximate numbers, instead of exact numbers

EXAMPLE: I don't need the exact numbers right now. Just give me some **back-of-the-envelope calculations**.

NOTE: This expression refers to the quick calculations one would do informally, as on the back of an envelope.

educated guess 根據經驗所作的推測
a guess based on experience; a piece of information based on prior knowledge, not hard facts or data

EXAMPLE: I'd say there are about a million potential consumers for your new line of cosmetics, but that's just an **educated guess**.

in hot water 惹禍上身
in trouble

EXAMPLE: Ian was **in hot water** with the government after he was caught making illegal copies of software.

(to) crunch the numbers 算出財務數字
to perform financial calculations

EXAMPLE: Reed Corporation is thinking about buying a small company. First, they'll need to **crunch the numbers** and see if their acquisition will be profitable.

NOTE: You will also see the noun form of this expression, "number cruncher," used to describe somebody who makes a lot of financial calculations as part of his or her job.

(it or that) blows my mind 令我頭大／頭疼
it bothers me; it really surprises me; it amazes me

EXAMPLE: **It blows my mind that** our company is trying to save money by taking away our free coffee service.

(to) run (the) numbers 計算財務數字
to perform financial calculations

EXAMPLE: Should we lease or buy the equipment? We'll need to **run the numbers** to help us make the decision.

in the red 虧損
losing money; when expenses are greater than revenues

EXAMPLE: We need to do something to start making profits. If we're **in the red** for one more quarter, we're going to go out of business.

NOTE: This expression comes from the accounting practice of marking debits (subtractions to the account) in red and credits (additions to the account) in black. The opposite of "in the red" is "in the black," meaning profitable.

one's head is on the chopping block　（某人）快被炒魷魚了

in a position where one is likely to be fired or get in trouble

EXAMPLE: After Earthy Foods released a frozen dinner that made many consumers sick, their CEO's **head was on the chopping block**.

NOTE: A chopping block is a piece of wood on which food or wood is chopped. Having your head on the block would suggest that it is going to be cut off. Fortunately, the meaning here is not literal. If your head is on the chopping block, you might lose your job, but at least you'll still have your head!

(to) give somebody the green light　通過／同意

to give permission to move forward with a project

EXAMPLE: Super Software's Moscow office has developed its own regional advertising campaign. They hope that headquarters in California will **give them the green light** to proceed with the campaign.

(to) break even　收支平衡

to make neither a profit or a loss; the point at which revenues equal costs

EXAMPLE: You **broke even** during your first year in business? That's good since most companies lose money during their first year.

(to) pull the plug　喊停／中止

to put a stop to a project or initiative, usually because it's not going well; to stop something from moving forward; to discontinue

EXAMPLE: After losing millions of dollars drilling for oil in Nebraska and finding nothing, the oil company finally **pulled the plug** on its exploration project.

ORIGIN: This expression refers to removing a plug to make something stop working — when you pull the plug out of the wall, your appliance doesn't work. In the 19th century, when this term originated, the plug was for a toilet. To flush the toilet, you had to pull out a plug.

✎ PRACTICE THE IDIOMS

Choose the most appropriate response to each sentence:

1) Did our CEO give the green light for the new project yet?
   a) No, he told us he needed more information before making a decision.
   b) Yes, he told us that the project was a bad idea and that we should stop working on it.
   c) Yes, he's going to discuss the project with his wife and see what she thinks.

2) Last year, our company made a loss on our new line of video games, but this year we'll break even.
   a) I'm sorry to hear you're broke.
   b) That's great. At least you're making progress.
   c) Too bad. Last year you did a lot better.

3) If you don't double-check those numbers and make sure they're correct, you might get in hot water with your boss.
   a) You're right. My boss always appreciates it when I give him the wrong numbers.
   b) That would be great. My boss enjoys soaking in hot water.
   c) You're right. My boss always gets angry when he finds mistakes.

4) Our company is in the red again this quarter.
   a) Congratulations! When's the celebration party?
   b) In the red again? I hope you don't go out of business!
   c) In the red? That's okay. It's better than being in the black.

5) We should pull the plug on our online advertising campaign.
   a) I agree. It's not bringing us any new business.
   b) I agree. Let's double our spending on it.
   c) I disagree. I think we should stop spending money on online advertising.

6) I know our company is looking for ways to cut costs. Do you think my head is on the chopping block?
   a) No, don't worry. They won't fire you.
   b) No, I don't think so. But you might get fired.
   c) No, I don't think they'll cut off your head.

7) Doesn't it blow your mind that they promoted Beth to General Manager after the mess she made in our department?
   a) Yes, she really deserved that promotion.
   b) No, but it does surprise me.
   c) Yes, it really surprises me!

8) Did you have a chance to crunch those numbers yet?
   a) Yes, I put them in a blender and crunched them up.
   b) Yes, I just put the financial reports on your desk.
   c) Yes, I'll take a look at them next week.

ANSWERS TO LESSON 2, p. 199

DISCUSSING A NEW AD CAMPAIGN
為新產品廣告作簡報

Ted works for an advertising agency. He's presenting to Sam and Lisa, who work for Pacific Beer Company.

Lisa: Ted would like to **run some ideas by us** for our new *ad campaign*.

Ted: Please **keep an open mind**. Remember that **nothing is set in stone** yet. We're still just **brainstorming**.

Sam: I hope that doesn't mean we're about to hear a lot of **half-baked ideas**!

Ted: I think you're going to like this. Our idea is to use a black bear as our *mascot*. Our **tagline** can be: "Strong enough to satisfy a bear."

Lisa: It would be great if people would *associate our brand with* a bear — strong and independent. That would really improve our *brand equity*.

Sam: I don't want to **throw cold water over** your idea, but where did you get the idea for a bear?

Ted: Didn't you hear about that bear at a campground a couple weeks ago? He entered a tent and drank two dozen Pacific beers! What a great *endorsement* for Pacific beer!

Lisa: I think we're **on the right track** with this campaign. The bear should **generate lots of buzz**. Everybody will be talking about the bear who loves Pacific beer!

Ted: And here's the **icing on the cake**: he won't demand **an arm and a leg** to **plug our product**. In fact, we can probably pay him in beer!

Sam: Okay, you've **twisted my arm**. Let's **run with the idea**.

Ted: Great. I'll **flesh it out** some more and **touch base with** you in a couple of days.

IDIOMS & EXPRESSIONS - LESSON 3

(to) run some ideas by someone 討論新構想
to discuss some new ideas

EXAMPLE: Our R&D department has some ideas about how to make our products safer. They'd like to meet this afternoon to **run some ideas by us**.

NOTE: You will also hear the singular form: to run an idea by someone.

(to) keep an open mind 敞開心胸
to be ready to accept new ideas and experiences

EXAMPLE: Cathy's new boss starts next Monday. She's heard he's very difficult to work with, but she's trying to **keep an open mind**.

nothing is set in stone 事情尚未定案
nothing is decided yet; things can still be changed

EXAMPLE: If you don't like the new product design, we can still change it. **Nothing is set in stone** yet.

(to) brainstorm 腦力激盪
to think up new ideas; to generate new ideas in a group

EXAMPLE: When the company started losing market share, the president called a meeting to **brainstorm** ways to turn around the business.

NOTE: There is also the expression "brainstorming session," in which a group gathers to come up with new ideas or to solve a problem.

16

half-baked idea   未成形的構想、想法
a stupid or impractical idea or suggestion

EXAMPLE: I can't believe we paid that consulting company so much money. We wanted them to help us grow our business and all they did was give us a bunch of **half-baked ideas**!

(to) throw cold water over (an idea, a plan)   潑冷水
to present reasons why something will not work; to discourage

EXAMPLE: Pat presented her boss with a plan to expand their business into China, but he **threw cold water over** her plan and told her to just focus on developing business in the United States.

NOTE: You will also hear the variation: to throw cold water on.

on the right track   （營運）方向正確
proceeding in a good way; going in the right direction

EXAMPLE: After years of struggling, Apple Computer is now **on the right track** by focusing on innovative products like the iPod.

(to) generate lots of buzz   引起大眾注意／造成話題
to cause many people to start talking about a product or service, usually in a positive way that increases sales

EXAMPLE: Procter & Gamble **generated lots of buzz** for its new toothpaste by giving away free samples to people on the streets of New York City.

NOTE: "Buzz" is a popular word for "attention."

icing on the cake   好上加好／更棒的是
an additional advantage; when one good thing happens, then another good thing happens along with it

EXAMPLE: Alison won $2 million in a sexual harassment lawsuit against her employer. And here's the **icing on the cake**: her company will have to pay all of her legal fees too!

NOTE: Icing is the creamy glaze put on top of a cake to decorate it and make it sweeter. The cake is already good enough — putting icing on top is something extra which makes it even better.

an arm and a leg 所費不貲／大筆費用
a lot of money

EXAMPLE: Jack always flies business class to Asia. The plane tickets cost **an arm and a leg**!

(to) plug (a product) 推銷產品／代言產品
to promote a product; to talk positively about a product

EXAMPLE: American Express often hires famous people to **plug their credit cards**. No wonder people pay attention to their ads!

(to) twist somebody's arm 說服
to convince somebody; to talk somebody into doing something

EXAMPLE: Ben didn't want to go to the company Christmas party this year, but Amy **twisted his arm** and he ended up having fun.

(to) run with an idea 採用構想
to proceed with an idea

EXAMPLE: After much discussion, the language school decided to **run with the idea** of offering a free class to each potential client.

(to) flesh out something 補充細節
to elaborate on something; to add more detail to a plan; to think in more detail about something

EXAMPLE: I like your idea of moving our manufacturing facility to China, but your plan doesn't have any details. Please **flesh out** your plan and present it at our board meeting next month.

(to) touch base with someone 聯絡
to get in contact with; to make brief contact with

EXAMPLE: "Hi, it's Andy calling from *City Style* magazine. I'm just **touching base with** you to see if you want to buy an ad."

---

tagline 口號
a slogan; a phrase used to promote a product

EXAMPLE: Meow Mix, a brand of cat food, has one of the best **taglines** in history: "Tastes so good, cats ask for it by name."

✍ PRACTICE THE IDIOMS

Choose the best substitute for the phrase or sentence in bold:

1) Starting a chain of coffee houses in Manhattan is **a half-baked idea**! There are already more than enough coffee houses in Manhattan.
   a) a great idea
   b) a really bad idea
   c) an idea that needs some more time in the oven

2) The government is discussing a new proposal to raise the minimum wage, but **nothing is set in stone yet**.
   a) nothing has been decided yet
   b) the proposal has been approved
   c) nothing will ever be decided

3) You don't have to **twist the boss's arm**. She's already decided to let everybody leave early on Friday to avoid holiday traffic.
   a) convince the boss
   b) hurt the boss
   c) ignore the boss

4) Arnold Schwarzenegger has appeared on television commercials in Japan, China, Austria, and Brazil, **plugging products** such as vitamin drinks and soup.
   a) drinking products
   b) advertising products
   c) terminating products

5) Before approaching a bank for a loan, you need to **flesh out** your business plan.
   a) throw out
   b) present
   c) add more detail to

6) Buying a new computer system would cost **an arm and a leg**. Let's just upgrade the system we already have.
   a) a lot of money
   b) not much money
   c) a lot of time

7) Paul and Susan make a good living running a bed-and-breakfast in Vermont. Meeting lots of friendly people is **the icing on the cake**.
   a) easy when you live in Vermont
   b) how they earn their living
   c) an additional benefit

8) I like your idea of selling our products by direct mail. **Let's run with it.**
   a) Let's discuss it further.
   b) Let's proceed with it.
   c) Let's forget it.

ANSWERS TO LESSON 3, p. 199

20

TALKING ABOUT MANUFACTURING
談論生產問題

Mike and Dan work for Swift Shoes, a manufacturer of sneakers. Mike is in charge of manufacturing. Dan is trying to push Mike to get some new shoes ready quickly.

Dan: We've decided to launch our new spring shoe on April 20th.

Mike: We're still trying to **work out the kinks** in our manufacturing process. Our factory in China is having trouble with the soles.

Dan: I know that, Mike. But you've still got three months. It should be plenty of time.

Mike: It could take another six months to **fine-tune** our manufacturing process.

Dan: Well, we don't have that much time. **No ifs, ands, or buts**, we need to launch on April 20th.

Mike: **Just for the record**, I think we're **cutting it a little close**. I recommend we launch on July 20th instead.

Dan: We can't. We've already decided on the **tagline**: "Spring into spring with Swift's new spring shoe."

Mike: It's time for a **reality check**. I'm telling you we might not be ready by April 20th, and you're telling me we have to be because of a **tagline**?

Dan: Mike, now's the time to **step up to the plate** and **get the job done**.

Mike: Well, I'm going to be working **down to the wire**.

Dan: Just **do whatever it takes**. Just make sure we've got a million pairs of shoes in *inventory* by the April 20th deadline.

Mike: I'm going to have to run the factories **24/7**. That's going to be a lot of *overtime pay*.

Dan: **At the end of the day**, a little extra expense doesn't matter. We just want those shoes ready by April 20th.

IDIOMS & EXPRESSIONS - LESSON 4

(to) work out the (or some) kinks　解決問題
to solve the problems with

EXAMPLE: The company announced that they will delay the launch of their new product by two weeks. They still need to **work out the kinks** with their packaging process.

NOTE: A "kink" is a problem or flaw in a system or plan.

. . . .

(to) fine-tune　稍作調整以達最佳狀態
to make small adjustments to something to increase the effectiveness or to make something work better

EXAMPLE: Rick hired an executive coach to help him **fine-tune** his managerial skills.

. . . .

no ifs, ands, or buts　沒有任何藉口／沒有但是、可是
no excuses; it's absolutely necessary that; this is how it's going to be no matter what anybody says

EXAMPLE: All employees must attend our team-building workshop tomorrow, **no ifs, ands, or buts**.

SYNONYM: no two ways about it

just for the record (also: for the record) 我再說清楚一點
let me make my opinion clear

EXAMPLE: I know that everybody else likes the idea of using a bear for a mascot, but, **just for the record**, I think it's a lousy idea.

(to) cut it (a little) close 太趕了
to try to do too much before a deadline; to not leave enough time to get a task done

EXAMPLE: Jerry promised his customer he'd ship out the farm equipment by the end of the week. Since we haven't assembled it yet, I think that's **cutting it close**.

tagline – see Lesson 3

reality check 醒醒吧／面對現實
let's think realistically about this situation (said when you don't like something that's being suggested because you don't think the other person is thinking practically or logically)

EXAMPLE: You think we can start selling our products through our website next month? Time for a **reality check**! Nobody at our company knows anything about e-commerce.

(to) step up to the plate 全力以赴／採取行動
to take action; to do one's best; to volunteer

EXAMPLE: We need somebody to be in charge of organizing the company holiday party. Who'd like to **step up to the plate** and start working on this project?

NOTE: This expression comes from baseball. You step up to the plate (a plastic mat on the ground) when it's your turn to hit the ball.

(to) get the job done 完成工作
to do the job successfully; to accomplish the task

EXAMPLE: We plan to outsource all of our software development to IBM. We know they have the resources to **get the job done**.

(to) work down to the wire   趕在最後一秒前完成／工作到最後一刻
to work until the last minute; to work until just before the deadline

EXAMPLE: The investment bankers need to turn in their report at 9 a.m. tomorrow morning, and they've still got many hours of work left on it. They're going to be working **down to the wire**.

NOTE: This expression comes from horse racing. In the 19th century, American racetracks placed wire across the track above the finish line. The wire helped determine which horse's nose crossed the line first. If a race was "down to the wire," it was a very close race, undecided until the very last second.

(to) do whatever it takes   盡其所能完成
to do anything and everything necessary to accomplish a task or reach a goal

EXAMPLE: It's very important that our new product be ready before Christmas. **Do whatever it takes** to make that happen.

24/7 (twenty-four seven)   馬不停蹄、夜以繼日／全年無休
around the clock; 24 hours a day, 7 days a week

EXAMPLE: During tax season, many accountants work **24/7**.

at the end of the day   總之
in summary; when we look back on this after we're finished

EXAMPLE: **At the end of the day**, the most important thing is how many cases of product we were able to ship this year.

NOTE: This expression is now overused. You will likely hear it, but you may not want to use it.

SYNONYM: when all is said and done

⚓ PRACTICE THE IDIOMS

Fill in the blanks, using the following idioms:

> working down to the wire
> get the job done
> cutting it close
> 24/7
> reality check
> fine-tuning
> work out the kinks
> does whatever it takes

Tom is a plant manager at Chocolate Delights, a manufacturer of chocolate. To prepare for the holiday season, the chocolate factory operates ____(1)____ and doesn't shut down for even an hour. Tom is very hardworking and every year ____(2)____ to get a large amount of chocolate produced to meet the holiday demand. This year, Chocolate Delights decided to make a new type of chocolate Santa Claus. There were some problems with the manufacturing process, but Tom was able to ____(3)____ . It was just a matter of ____(4)____ one of the machines. Tom's goal is to have 100,000 boxes of chocolate ready to ship by November 1. Will he reach this goal? Probably, but he'll be ____(5)____. Nancy, Tom's boss, is afraid he's ____(6)____ this year. "Time for a ____(7)____ ," she told him this morning. "If you don't speed up production, you're not going to reach your quota." Tom just smiled and replied, "Don't worry, I'll ____(8)____. You can count on me."

ANSWERS TO LESSON 4, p. 199

Our latest model cell phone was a real dog.

TALKING ABOUT COMPANY STRATEGY
談論公司策略

Andy and Laura work for Saltonica, a maker of cell phones. Sales have been slow lately, so Andy is recommending the company adopt a new strategy.

Andy: My team has come up with a new strategy. We can't continue being **fast followers**. We need to start developing our own **cutting-edge** technologies.

Laura: Why? We've been **fast followers** for the past ten years. **Why mess with success?**

Andy: Success? **Get with the program**. Our sales are way down. Our **cash cow**, the Model 8B, only sold 900 units last month!

Laura: I can understand why. That phone's a *relic*. It's been around for over three years. What about our new phones?

Andy: Our latest model cell phone was a **real dog**! It sold only 20 percent of our sales *forecast*.

Laura: Any idea why?

Andy: *Product life cycles* are much shorter now than before. New technologies are developed at a much faster rate.

Laura: So what are we supposed to do?

Andy: We need to become much more *innovative* as a company. Instead of producing **me-too products**, we need to **leapfrog our competitors**.

Laura: How do we do that?

Andy: **For starters**, we need to **beef up** our *R&D* department. We need to develop *differentiated products* which we can sell **at a premium**.

Laura: As a next step, let's **get buy-in** from our marketing and sales directors.

Andy: Right. We should get everyone **on the same page**.

IDIOMS & EXPRESSIONS - LESSON 5

fast followers　不創新只會亦步亦趨模仿競爭者的公司
a company that doesn't come up with new ideas or concepts first, but rather quickly copies those of other companies

EXAMPLE: Many PC manufacturers don't spend much on R&D. They are **fast followers**, waiting for competitors to innovate and then quickly copying their products.

cutting-edge　尖端／嶄新
very modern; using the latest technologies

EXAMPLE: Sony focuses on innovation and is known for its **cutting-edge** electronic goods.

Why mess with success?　何不撿現成的便宜？／現在做得不錯何必改變？
Why start doing things differently when the way we're doing them now is working?

EXAMPLE: We could move our manufacturing plant to China, but we're doing very well manufacturing in the United States. **Why mess with success?**

(to) get with the program 睜大眼睛看看現狀
to pay attention to what's going on right now; to be alert to what's happening now

EXAMPLE: **Get with the program**. Our competitors have all started to outsource their call centers to India to save money, while we're still paying a fortune here in the United States!

cash cow 主力商品／主要獲利商品
a product, service, or business division that generates a lot of cash for the company, without requiring much investment

EXAMPLE: With strong sales every year and a great brand name, Mercedes is a **cash cow** for DaimlerChrysler.

real dog 失敗的產品
a bad product; a commercial failure

EXAMPLE: In 1985, the Coca-Cola Company released New Coke. It was a **real dog** and was in stores for only a few months.

me-too products 相似的產品
products that are extremely similar to another company's products; copies

EXAMPLE: Procter & Gamble is a company famous for innovation. They rarely produce **me-too products**.

(to) leapfrog one's competitors 超越同業
to make a product that is technologically superior to competitors' products

EXAMPLE: Logitech introduced a product that **leapfrogged its competitors**: a mouse that was both wireless and *ergonomic*.

NOTE: Leapfrog is a popular children's game in which one child bends down and another jumps over him or her.

for starters 第一步
as a first step; to begin with

EXAMPLE: You want to do business in Russia? **For starters**, I'd recommend setting up an office in Moscow.

(to) beef up 改善加強
to improve; to add to

EXAMPLE: Leave plenty of extra time at the airport. Ever since they **beefed up** security, it takes a long time to get through the lines.

at a premium 走高價位
at a high price; at a relatively high price

EXAMPLE: When flat-screen televisions first came out, they were selling **at a premium.**

(to) get buy-in (from) 得到支持、同意
to get agreement or approval from

EXAMPLE: To be an effective leader, you need to **get buy-in** for your decisions from employees throughout the organization.

(to be) on the same page 觀念一致
to be in agreement; when everybody has the latest information on what's going on

EXAMPLE: Before we start on the next phase of this project, let's have a meeting and make sure everybody's **on the same page**.

NOTE: This expression is overused. You will likely hear it, but you may not want to use it.

✎ PRACTICE THE IDIOMS

Choose the best substitute for the phrase or sentence in bold:

1) Mattel, a large toy company, always **beefs up** its advertising around the holiday season.
   a) changes
   b) increases
   c) decreases

2) Amazon.com uses **cutting-edge** technologies to determine which products each of its customers is most likely to buy.
   a) sharp
   b) inexpensive
   c) the most modern

3) We need to re-design our entire store. **For starters**, we should move the cash register from the back of the store to the front of the store.
   a) as a final step
   b) as a first priority
   c) for people who can't find the cash register now

4) Your company is introducing garlic fruitcake? **That sounds like a real dog!**
   a) What a great idea!
   b) That sounds like a terrible idea!
   c) I'm sure dogs will love it!

5) After Apple's iPod proved to be successful, several other manufacturers came out with **me-too products**.
   a) products very similar to the iPod
   b) their own innovative products
   c) products very different from the iPod

6) Your plan is good, but before you proceed, you'll need to **get buy-in** from the company president.
   a) get a purchase order
   b) get approval
   c) get a promotion

7) With our new solar-powered automobile, we're going to **leapfrog our competitors**.
   a) make all our competition disappear
   b) turn our competitors into small green animals
   c) come out with a superior product

8) You don't own a cell phone? I thought everybody had one. You need **to get with the program**!
   a) get a program to teach you how to use the phone
   b) join a cell phone calling plan that offers unlimited minutes
   c) get a cell phone too, so you're not missing what everyone else has

ANSWERS TO LESSON 5, p. 199

REVIEW FOR LESSONS 1-5

Fill in the blank with the missing word:

1) Steve won't be satisfied with a simple digital camera. He wants one with all the _____ and whistles.

   a) widgets   b) bells   c) chimes

2) I know you're planning on spending your entire advertising budget on TV advertising. _____ for the record, I don't think that's a good idea.

   a) just   b) only   c) simply

3) HBO _____ up with a winner with its popular show *Sex and the City*. It became an international hit.

   a) came   b) thought   c) arrived

4) Jack didn't want to buy laptops for everybody in the office, but the office manager succeeded in twisting his _____.

   a) leg   b) mind   c) arm

5) After two years on the market, this product is still not selling well. I think we should _____ the plug.

   a) push   b) remove   c) pull

6) Our president has made it very clear that we need to double our revenues this year. No _____, ands, or buts.

   a) ifs   b) howevers   c) maybes

7) We don't have any job openings right now, but please _____ base with us in a couple of months.

   a) reach   b) contact   c) touch

8) Irene would like to start a business from her home, but she's not sure how to go _____ it.

   a) around   b) about   c) with

9) Some of your colleagues might not like you, but at the _____ of the day, what really matters is what your boss thinks of you.

   a) end   b) close   c) finish

10) When it was clear that the new product was a failure, nobody was willing to step up to the _____ and take responsibility.

   a) table   b) plate   c) dish

11) Holiday time is very busy at the department store, so the store is planning on beefing _____ its sales staff for the entire month of December.

   a) out   b) over   c) up

12) Charlie loves his job, so when he won the employee-of-the- year award, it was just _____ on the cake.

   a) frosting   b) icing   c) candles

13) Don't tell Tony we're planning a retirement party for him. It's going to be a surprise. _____ the word!

   a) Sister's   b) Dad's   c) Mum's

14) After another bad quarter, the president's head was on the _____.

   a) cutting board   b) chopping block c) operating table

15) General Electric is thinking about selling off one of its businesses in India, but nothing is set in _____ yet.

   a) stone   b) rock   c) paper

ANSWERS TO REVIEW, p. 200

Kudos to Linda!

DISCUSSING GOOD RESULTS
討論良好績效

Peter, Linda, and Todd work as managers at Capital City Bank, a retail bank. Linda's creative idea for attracting new customers to the bank has generated lots of new business.

Peter: Great news! We had a **record-breaking** quarter. We brought in revenues of $500,000.

Linda: Wow, revenues really were **though the roof**!

Todd: That's great. **Kudos to** Linda! She deserves a **pat on the back**. The **guerrilla marketing** campaign she **dreamed up** was brilliant. She sent out e-mail to all of our customers asking them to e-mail a friend about our services. For each friend they e-mailed, they received a free gift.

Peter: Linda, your campaign helped us **drum up a lot of business**. We **signed on 800 new customers**.

Linda: I'm really glad my plan **panned out**. I thought it would, since everybody loves a *freebie!*

Todd: Linda, we can always count on you to **think outside the box**.

Linda: **For the record**, Peter helped me come up with the idea.

Peter: Thanks for **sharing the credit**, Linda. But it was your idea.

Todd: The important thing is that we're now giving our biggest competitor, U.S. Bank, **a run for their money**.

record-breaking　破紀錄
better than ever before; exceeding all previous results

EXAMPLE: After another **record-breaking** quarter, eBay's stock price hit a new high.

though the roof　高於原先的預期
very high; higher than expected

EXAMPLE: No wonder people are complaining about the cost of heating their homes. Oil prices have gone **through the roof**!

kudos to　歸功於／掌聲鼓勵……
I'd like to give credit to; I'd like to acknowledge

EXAMPLE: **Kudos to** our R&D department. They've come up with a new shampoo formula that's cheaper to manufacture and more effective on damaged hair.

NOTE: Kudos is the Greek word for "praise."

a pat on the back　讚揚
credit; recognition; praise

EXAMPLE: "Team, give yourselves **a pat on the back**. Our results are in and we just had our most successful quarter ever!"

guerrilla marketing　創新的行銷手法
innovative methods to sell products; non-traditional methods of advertising or promotion that deliver good results with minimal spending

EXAMPLE: To promote his new Internet dating service, Don painted his car pink and wrote "Don's Dating Service" in big letters on both sides of the car. That's effective **guerrilla marketing**!

NOTE: The word "guerrilla" refers to carrying on a war using independent bands of soldiers, who tend to use very aggressive and non-traditional tactics to win battles.

36

dream up 構想出

to think up something creative or unusual; to come up with an original idea; to invent

EXAMPLE: A disposable lemon-scented toilet brush? What will companies **dream up** next?

. . . .

(to) drum up business 創造業績

to create business; to find new customers

EXAMPLE: Sales have been very slow lately. Do you have any ideas for **drumming up business**?

. . . .

(to) sign on new customers (or members) 增加新會員

to enlist new customers; to get customers to open an account or take a membership

EXAMPLE: The fitness center was able to **sign on 300 new members** in May thanks to their successful advertising campaign.

. . . .

(to) pan out 成功

to succeed; to bring the desired results

EXAMPLE: When Steve's career in acting didn't **pan out**, he decided to go to business school.

. . . .

(to) think outside the box 思考跳脫窠臼

to think creatively; to think in a new and different way

EXAMPLE: : The small law firm is losing business to larger rivals. The firm needs to **think outside the box** and come up with some creative ways to market its services.

NOTE: This expression is now overused. You will likely hear it, but you may not want to use it.

ORIGIN: This phrase refers to a puzzle used by consultants in the 1970s and 1980s. To solve it, you must connect nine dots, using four straight lines drawn continuously. Your pen must never leave the paper. (The only solution to this puzzle is to draw lines outside the border of the box. Therefore, you must "think outside the box" to solve the puzzle).

for the record
see Lesson 4

....

(to) share the credit 將功勞歸於……

to acknowledge someone else's contribution; to share with somebody else recognition for a job well done

EXAMPLE: Thank you for giving me the award for coming up with the best new product idea this year. But I really need to **share the credit** with my colleagues in the marketing department.

....

(a) run for one's money 來勢洶洶、強勁的競爭

strong competition

EXAMPLE: When Yahoo decided to go into the online search business, they gave Google a **run for their money**.

ORIGIN: This expression comes from the world of horse racing. It refers to a horse on which one has bet money and which comes close to winning but doesn't win.

✍ PRACTICE THE IDIOMS

Choose the most appropriate response to each sentence:

1) Our store had a very successful holiday season this year. Sales were through the roof!
   a) I'm sorry to hear that you need a new roof.
   b) That's great. Congratulations!
   c) Don't worry. Maybe next year will be better.

2) We're looking for some fresh thinking in our marketing department. Are you good at thinking outside the box?
   a) Yes, I tend to think like everybody else.
   b) Yes, I enjoy approaching new projects in a traditional way.
   c) Yes, I'm great at coming up with new and creative ideas.

3) I'd like to share the credit with you. Without you, I wouldn't have been able to find this important new client.
   a) Thank you. I appreciate the recognition.
   b) Thanks, but I already have enough credit.
   c) I think I deserve some of the credit too.

4) A big Ace Hardware store is opening up in town. Do you think they'll give our local hardware store a run for their money?
   a) Definitely. Their selection will be bigger and their prices may be lower.
   b) Yes, our local hardware store will definitely run out of money.
   c) No. Everybody in town will start shopping at Ace Hardware.

5) Since you need to drum up some new business, I suggest you exhibit at a trade show.
   a) We don't have any business right now.
   b) We've been thinking about going into the drum business.
   c) Great idea! I'm sure we could find some new clients there.

6) You deserve a pat on the back for figuring out how to fix our computer network.
   a) Thanks. It was my pleasure.
   b) Thanks. Let me turn around so you can see my back.
   c) Sorry. I wish I could've done a better job.

7) Kudos to you and the rest of the manufacturing department for figuring out how to cut our production costs!
   a) We don't need any more kudos. We have enough in inventory.
   b) Thank you. We are proud of our results.
   c) We'll try our best, but we can't guarantee anything.

8) Traditional ways of advertising are no longer working for our firm. Do you think we should try some guerrilla marketing?
   a) Absolutely. It's always better to use reliable old methods.
   b) Yes, new ways of marketing might help increase sales.
   c) No, I think you should try marketing to monkeys instead.

ANSWERS TO LESSON 6, p. 200

We're in deep trouble. Sales are down by 50 percent.

DISCUSSING BAD RESULTS
討論失敗案例

Ron, Alex, and Pam work for Brooklyn Brewski, a company that brews and distributes beer throughout New York. The company's recent results have been terrible.

Alex: We need to **face the music** here. We're **in deep trouble**! Sales are down by 50 percent versus last year.

Pam: It looks like we're going to be **in the red** for the year **to the tune of** $1 million.

Ron: **No wonder**. We're losing **market share** to Manhattan Beer.

Alex: Why? We need to **get to the bottom of** this!

Pam: Every year they come up with new beers. They're really **on top of trends**. For instance, last year they released a *low-carb* beer.

Ron: **No wonder** they're **eating our lunch**! They're **cashing in on** the latest trends and **bringing great new products to market**.

Pam: Meanwhile, we're **running in place**. We need a new *product line* and new ideas for marketing.

Alex: It's time to **clean house** and bring some **new blood** into this company.

Ron: **You took the words right out of my mouth!** We need some new people with fresh ideas.

(to) face the music　面對現實

to admit that there's a problem; to deal with an unpleasant situation realistically

EXAMPLE: Enron executives finally had to **face the music** and admit that they were involved in some illegal activities.

in deep trouble　有大麻煩了

having a serious problem; in crisis

EXAMPLE: If there's another winter without any snowfall, Craig's snow plowing business is going to be **in deep trouble**.

in the red

see Lesson 2

to the tune of (followed by a number)　大約的數目是⋯⋯

in the amount of; approximately

EXAMPLE: This year, our Beijing office will bring in revenues **to the tune of** two million dollars.

no wonder　難怪

it's not surprising that

EXAMPLE: **No wonder** Randy hasn't been promoted in 10 years. He just sits in his office surfing the Internet all day.

market share　市佔率

the percentage of sales a company has in relation to its competitors for a product or product line

EXAMPLE: We're in trouble. Our **market share** went from 50 percent last year to only 20 percent this year!

NOTE: Here are the verbs most frequently associated with the phrase market share:

(to) gain market share　增加市佔率

to increase one's share of the market

EXAMPLE: With the launch of their popular new herbal toothpaste, Colgate **gained market share**.

(to) lose market share 減少市佔率
to decrease one's share of the market

EXAMPLE: Last year, Internet Explorer **lost market share** to one of its rivals, Mozilla.

(to) steal market share (from) 搶生意
to take sales away from a competitor

EXAMPLE: Motorola and Samsung are trying to **steal market share from** Nokia.

(to) get to the bottom of something 發現問題的源頭／追根究柢
to figure out what's going on; to find out what's causing a problem

EXAMPLE: When hundreds of people had heart attacks after taking Zylestra's new prescription drug, the Federal Drug Administration promised to **get to the bottom of it**.

on top of trends 領先潮流
modern; aware and responding to the latest tastes

EXAMPLE: The Gap is **on top of trends**. They always have the latest styles in their stores.

eating one's lunch 搶走⋯⋯的生意
taking away one's business

EXAMPLE: Ever since Wal-Mart came into town, our local stores have been doing poorly. Wal-Mart is **eating their lunch**.

(to) cash in on 靠⋯⋯賺錢
to make money on; to benefit financially from

EXAMPLE: Jamie Oliver, star of the TV show *The Naked Chef*, **cashed in on** his popularity by writing cookbooks and opening restaurants.

(to) bring a product to market 開發新產品
to introduce or launch a new product

EXAMPLE: Next year will be very busy for Procter & Gamble's Oil of Olay division. They're going to **bring many new products to market**.

(to) run in place 遇到瓶頸

to not make any progress; to be stuck; to remain in the same place for a long period of time

EXAMPLE: Our company needs to come up with some innovative new products. We've been **running in place** for years.

. . . .

(to) clean house 人事精簡／裁員

to fire a lot of employees

EXAMPLE: The airline was nearly bankrupt. They had no choice but to **clean house**.

. . . .

new blood 新血／新進員工

new employees

EXAMPLE: When the biotech company brought some **new blood** into their R&D department, their business really started to improve.

. . . .

You took the words right out of my mouth! 我也這麼認為

I completely agree with you; I was just going to say that

EXAMPLE: "I hope the boss doesn't hold our holiday party at his house again this year." — "**You took the words right out of my mouth!** I'd much rather go to a restaurant."

✎ PRACTICE THE IDIOMS

Fill in the blanks using the following idioms:

> **new blood**
> **in deep trouble**
> **no wonder**
> **running in place**
> **eating their lunch**
> **face the music**
> **on top of trends**
> **bring some new products to market**

Zylestra is a large pharmaceutical company. They haven't introduced any major new drugs in a long time. They've been _____(1)_____ for the past few years. Their biggest competitor, Delmar Drugs, is stealing market share from them and is _____(2)_____. It's really _____(3)_____ Delmar is more successful. Over the past few years, they've come out with effective drugs for lowering cholesterol and reducing the risk of heart disease. Delmar understands what their customers want. They invest heavily in consumer research to stay _____(4)_____. Meanwhile, Zylestra is still selling the same drugs it was selling three years ago. If Zylestra doesn't follow Delmar's example and _____(5)_____ soon, they're going to be _____(6)_____. Investors in the company hope that Richard Pierce, Zylestra's CEO, will _____(7)_____ and take action to turn around the company. As a first step, he might consider bringing in some _____(8)_____ to help him run the company.

ANSWERS TO LESSON 7, p. 200

I recommend we bite the bullet and move our operations to China.

DISCUSSING A DIFFICULT DECISION
討論困難的決策

Anna, Lynn, and Jeff are thinking about moving their manufacturing facilities from the United States to China. Jeff is having trouble deciding what to do.

Anna: We need to decide already whether or not we want to move our manufacturing from the United States to China. Jeff, have you made the final decision?

Jeff: There are *pros and cons* to moving it to China. I've been **back and forth on this issue** for months. I'm **of two minds**.

Anna: Jeff, I know this is a **tough call**, but now is not the time to be **wishy-washy**. We need to make a decision.

Lynn: That's right, and I recommend we **bite the bullet** and move our operations to China.

Anna: Or we could **test the waters** by moving 25 percent of our operations there.

Lynn: Good idea. That would give us **the best of both worlds**: we could reduce our risk, while starting to enjoy some of the cost savings from lower-cost manufacturing.

Jeff: I agree with you that we should **put a stake in the ground**. Let's move a quarter of our operations to China.

Lynn: **Good call**, Jeff!

Jeff: I hope I don't **live to regret this decision**.

Anna: You won't. **My gut tells me** we're doing the right thing.

IDIOMS & EXPRESSIONS - LESSON 8

back and forth on an issue 搖擺不定
repeatedly changing one's mind about something; having trouble settling on an opinion or decision

EXAMPLE: Should we change our company health care plan? I can't make up my mind. I go **back and forth on the issue**.

......

of two minds 掙扎不已
conflicted; having conflicting ideas about something

EXAMPLE: Many consumers are **of two minds** about buying organic produce. On the one hand, it is often more expensive than regular produce. On the other hand, it may be healthier.

......

tough call 困難的決定
a difficult decision; something difficult to predict

EXAMPLE: It was a **tough call**, but the company finally decided to close its factory in South Carolina.

......

wishy-washy 優柔寡斷
ineffective; lacking will-power; indecisive; incapable of making clear decisions

EXAMPLE: Wendy is very **wishy-washy**. She changed her mind a hundred times about which packaging design to use for the new product.

......

(to) bite the bullet 痛下決定
to make a difficult or painful decision; to take a difficult step

EXAMPLE: When demand was down, U.S. automakers had to **bite the bullet** and cut jobs.

ORIGIN: This idiom comes from the military. During the Civil War in the United States, doctors sometimes ran out of whiskey for killing the pain. A bullet would be put in the wounded soldier's mouth during surgery. He would "bite the bullet" to distract him from the pain and keep him quiet so the doctor could do his work in peace.

(to) test the waters 試做（以探知後果）

to try something out before committing to it; to see what the response or outcome will be to an intended action

EXAMPLE: Before quitting his job as a lawyer to become a chef, Chad **tested the waters** by working weekends at a restaurant.

the best of both worlds 雙邊得利

a situation or product that offers two very different advantages at the same time

EXAMPLE: BMW's new sports car offers **the best of both worlds**: a reliable car that's also fun to drive.

(to) put a stake in the ground 跨出第一步

to take the first step; to make a big move to get something started; to make a commitment

EXAMPLE: Our business in California has grown steadily over the past two years. Now is the time to **put a stake in the ground** and open a regional office there.

good call 好決定
good decision

EXAMPLE: **Good call** on buying Google stock. It has gone way up since you bought it.

(to) live to regret a decision 懊悔所下的決定
to feel bad later about one's decision

EXAMPLE: The mayor agreed to allow a new dump to be built in town, but he later **lived to regret his decision**.

my gut tells me 我有強烈的預感
I have a strong feeling that; my intuition tells me

EXAMPLE: It's true that I don't know him well, but **my gut tells me** that James is the right person for the sales director position.

NOTE: The "gut" is both the intestines and stomach and also the innermost emotional response.

Choose the best substitute for the phrase or sentence in bold:

1) Sandra **is of two minds about** leaving her job to get an MBA.
   a) is upset about
   b) isn't sure about
   c) is very positive about

2) You decided to invest some money in real estate? **Good call!**
   a) You're a good person!
   b) I'll call you back!
   c) Good idea!

3) Ford Motor Company debated for a long time whether or not to start making cars in Russia, but the company finally decided to **bite the bullet**.
   a) drop the project
   b) go ahead with it
   c) enter the weapons business

4) I know you're nervous about the launch of our new robotic vacuum cleaner, but **my gut tells me** it's going to be a big seller.
   a) I have a strong feeling that
   b) my friend tells me that
   c) I don't think that

5) Janet left her old job before finding a new one and **lived to regret her decision**.
   a) had trouble finding a new job
   b) was happy with her decision
   c) was sorry about it later

6) Unfortunately, our company president is not a great leader. He's **wishy-washy**.
   a) inconsiderate
   b) not good at making decisions
   c) lazy

7) Kate says running a business from her home **gives her the best of both worlds**: she can stay at home with her four young children and still make some money.
   a) allows her all possible advantages
   b) gives her more work than she can handle
   c) lets her stay at home all day doing nothing

8) The computer store was unsure at first how much demand there would be for the new line of laptops, so they started with a small order to **test the waters**.
   a) make sure the laptops really worked
   b) see if there was demand for the laptops
   c) see if customers were interested in buying water

ANSWERS TO LESSON 8, p. 200

This website is a far cry from what we were expecting.

DEALING WITH A DISSATISFIED CUSTOMER
處理顧客申訴

John hired Kevin's web design firm to design a website for his company, but John's not satisfied with the end result.

John: We're disappointed with the website you designed for us. It's **a far cry from** what we were expecting.

Kevin: I'm sorry you're not satisfied. We really **went all out** to make it a great site.

John: Well, I'm not going to **mince words**. You charged us a **pretty penny**, and you didn't **deliver**.

Kevin: Wow, I'm really surprised to hear you say that! We **pulled out all the stops**.

John: Don't try to **pull the wool over my eyes**. You promised that your best people would work on this project, but our website looks like it was designed by a *summer intern!*

Kevin: What exactly is the problem with the site?

John: **Where to begin?** The *shopping cart* doesn't even work.

Kevin: Really? Well, we'll **get right on that.**

John: And you guys **messed around** forever getting the site done. You were three months behind schedule!

Kevin: I'm sorry about that. We were **swamped**. Let me **make it up to you**. We'll give you a 25 percent discount on the project.

a far cry from 差距太大／出入太大

different than; not at all like; much less than

EXAMPLE: Cisco Systems' stock may be trading higher, but it's still **a far cry from** where it was in 2000.

(to) go all out 盡力

to make a big effort; to try hard

EXAMPLE: The small gift shop **went all out** on advertising in December, trying to increase its holiday sales.

(to) mince words 修飾詞藻

to control one's language so as to be polite

EXAMPLE: Sue told you your new product idea was "the stupidest idea she's ever heard?" Clearly she's not one to **mince words**!

NOTE: Mince has two main meanings: in this expression, it means "to make less harsh." It also means "to chop foods into tiny pieces."

pretty penny 一大筆錢

a lot of money; too much money (when referring to the cost of something)

EXAMPLE: Ruth made a **pretty penny** selling antiques on eBay.

(to) deliver 完成任務／達到預期目標（水準）

to meet expectations or requirements of a task, project, or job

EXAMPLE: You made a lot of promises during your job interview here. Now that you're hired, I hope you can **deliver**!

(to) pull out all the stops 用盡全力／想方設法

to use all one's resources to get something done; to try very hard

EXAMPLE: Many airline companies are **pulling out all the stops** to win the right to fly direct to China.

ORIGIN: This expression comes from the world of music. To increase the volume of a pipe organ, organists pull out stops (levers that control the volume).

(to) pull the wool over one's eyes　把⋯⋯矇在鼓裡／欺騙
to deceive someone

EXAMPLE: Are you telling me the truth or are you trying to **pull the wool over my eyes**?

ORIGIN: In in the 17th and 18th centuries, men sometimes wore wigs. The "wool" refers to the wig (made of wool). Pulling the wool over the eyes made it impossible to see.

Where to begin?　千頭萬緒不知從何說起
There is so much to say, I have to think about where to start (usually used when you're about to complain and you want to stress that there's a lot to complain about).

EXAMPLE: Your new marketing campaign has so many problems. **Where to begin?**

(to) get right on something　馬上著手處理
to take care of something immediately

EXAMPLE: You need my help in finding a new office to lease? I'll **get right on that**.

(to) mess around　混水摸魚
to waste time; to spend time with no particular purpose or goal

EXAMPLE: We don't have time to **mess around** with the design for the packaging. Let's just design it quickly and get it into production!

(to be) swamped　有太多工作／忙不過來
to have too much work to do; to be extremely busy

EXAMPLE: Accounting firms are **swamped** during tax season.

(to) make it up to you　補償
to do something to compensate you for your trouble

EXAMPLE: I'm sorry that you weren't happy with the sign we made for your business. Let me **make it up to you** and make a new sign for you at no charge.

Fill in the blanks, using the following idioms:

> mince words
> pull the wool over my eyes
> make it up to you
> a far cry from
> pretty penny
> pulled out all the stops
> deliver
> Where to begin

Linda: We're never going to use Donna's Delights Catering again! You promised you'd do a great job with our holiday party, but you didn't _____(1)_____ .

Donna: Oh, really? What exactly was the problem?

Linda: _____(2)_____ ? There were so many problems! First of all, the main course was _____(3)_____ what we were expecting. I'm not going to _____(4)_____ . The steak you served us tasted like rubber!

Donna: I'm really surprised. I put my best chef on this project, and we bought the best steak available. We _____(5)_____ .

Linda: I have a feeling you're trying to _____(6)_____ . I know my steak, and I know the steak you served was low quality.

Donna: Well, I guess it's possible we ordered the wrong meat.

Linda: You charged us a _____(7)_____ for your services, and you did a lousy job. We won't be using your company anymore.

Donna: I'm sorry. Let me _____(8)_____ . We'll bring free lunch for your entire office next Friday.

ANSWERS TO LESSON 9, p. 200

DISCUSSING A DIFFICULT REQUEST
討論執行上的困難

Tanya is head of R&D in a laboratory for Sudsco, a company that makes shampoo. Here she meets with colleagues John and Andy to discuss a request from the marketing department.

Tanya: Let me **kick off** this meeting with some news. Our marketing department would like us to produce a new fragrance by the end of next month.

John: Oh, brother.* We **need this extra work like a hole in the head**! What fragrance are they looking for?

Tanya: Mango.

Andy: Mango? Are they out of their minds? Do they know how *tough* that is?

Tanya: Yeah, but I told them we'd **take a crack at it**. If we **put our minds to it**, I know we can do it.

Andy: I don't know. It's not going to be easy.

Tanya: Let's **roll up our sleeves** and **give it our best shot**. **Nothing ventured, nothing gained**.

John: Well, Tanya, you certainly have a **can-do attitude**!

Tanya: Actually, this is **child's play** compared to what our CEO wants us to do by the end of the year. He wants us to come up with new, improved formulas for all 50 of our shampoos.

Andy: What? How are we supposed to manage that? Sometimes I think the **bigwigs** at this company are **out of touch with reality**!

* oh, brother – a polite way of expressing annoyance

IDIOMS & EXPRESSIONS - LESSON 10

(to) kick of 開始
to start something, such as a meeting or a project

EXAMPLE: Bill Gates **kicked off** the conference by showing a demonstration of Microsoft's new search engine.

NOTE: You will also see the phrase "kick-off meeting," meaning the first meeting to get a new project started.

(to) need something like a hole in the head ⋯⋯不是某人所樂見的
to have no need for something; to have no desire for something

EXAMPLE: One of our competitors is threatening to take us to court. We **need that like a hole in the head**!

out of one's mind 瘋了
crazy; having unrealistic thoughts or ideas

EXAMPLE: Our DSL provider is telling us that our rates will soon go up by 50 percent. Are they **out of their minds**?

(to) take a crack at something 試試看
to try something

EXAMPLE: It's going to be hard for us to lower our raw materials cost on this product, but we'll **take a crack at it**.

SYNONYM: to have a go at something

(to) put one's mind to something 全心投入／全力以赴
to focus on a task; to try hard to do something

EXAMPLE: Your accounting course may be difficult, but if you **put your mind to it**, you'll get through it.

58

(to) roll up one's sleeves　捲起袖子，準備工作
to get ready to start something; to prepare to do something

EXAMPLE: We've got to pack up 500 crystal vases by tomorrow morning, so let's **roll up our sleeves** and get to work.

....

(to) give it one's best shot　盡全力／全力以赴
to make one's best effort to get something done; to try to do something, even though you're not sure if you'll be successful

EXAMPLE: The small brewery went out of business after three unprofitable years, but at least they **gave it their best shot**.

....

nothing ventured, nothing gained　不入虎穴焉得虎子／不試怎知有無
If you don't try to do something, you'll never succeed.

EXAMPLE: It's risky to spend so much money developing a new brand, but **nothing ventured, nothing gained**.

....

can-do attitude　樂觀積極的態度
a positive way of looking at things; an optimistic perspective; a positive attitude

EXAMPLE: Marie always says that nothing's impossible. She's got a real **can-do attitude**.

....

child's play　雕蟲小技／簡單任務
an easy task

EXAMPLE: Evan has been an auto mechanic for 20 years, so replacing your windshield wipers will be **child's play** for him.

....

bigwig　頭頭／上頭的人
very important person; person in charge

EXAMPLE: All the **bigwigs** from the company went to Hawaii for a four-day conference.

SYNONYM: head honcho; big cheese; VIP (very important person)

ORIGIN: This term comes from "big wig" — the large wigs that English men wore in the 17th and 18th centuries. Men of great importance wore the biggest wigs.

out of touch with reality 脫離現實／搞不清現實
unrealistic; not aware of what's really going on

> EXAMPLE: The CEO believes his company's stock price will triple in a year. Most people think he's **out of touch with reality**.

✒ PRACTICE THE IDIOMS

Choose the best substitute for the phrase or sentence in bold:

1) Our president gave everybody business card holders for Christmas. **I need another business card holder like a hole in the head.**
   a) I really need a new business card holder.
   b) I'm happy to get another business card holder.
   c) I really don't need another business card holder.

2) Installing that new computer software was **child's play** for Mark. He's got a PhD in computer science.
   a) very easy
   b) challenging
   c) enjoyable

3) I agree with you that we may not be successful entering the market in China, but **nothing ventured, nothing gained**.
   a) we should take a risk and enter the Chinese market
   b) we shouldn't enter the Chinese market
   c) if we enter the Chinese market, we'll definitely succeed

4) If you can't figure out how to fix the jammed printer, let Adam **take a crack at it**.
   a) fix the crack in it
   b) try to fix it
   c) throw it in the trash

5) The company **kicked off** the new fiscal year by announcing several exciting new products.
   a) ended
   b) postponed
   c) began

6) It won't be easy, but if you **put your mind to it**, you can study for your law degree while also working full-time.
   a) don't think too much about it
   b) work hard at it
   c) think about it

7) Sorry I couldn't get you the financial reports by Friday. I **gave it my best shot**, but I just couldn't finish on time.
   a) tried as hard as I could
   b) made a little effort
   c) didn't try too hard

8) If you want to work for IBM, call my cousin Alan. He's a **bigwig** there.
   a) low-level employee
   b) frequent visitor
   c) senior executive

ANSWERS TO LESSON 10, p. 200

REVIEW FOR LESSONS 6-10

Fill in the blank with the missing word:

1) We're not happy with our accounting firm. All of the mistakes they made with our taxes cost us a pretty _____.

    a) nickel   b) penny   c) dollar

2) If the pharmaceutical company's new product is not approved by the Food and Drug Administration, they're going to be _____ deep trouble.

    a) with   b) on   c) in

3) Sales will probably be slow after the holidays. Let's think of a way to _____ up some business.

    a) beat   b) break   c) drum

4) Olivia is _____ two minds about quitting her job and starting her own business. On the one hand, it will be more exciting. On the other hand, she's afraid of taking a risk.

    a) of   b) with   c) at

5) In the months following Google's initial public offering, the stock price went _____ the roof.

    a) up   b) out   c) through

6) Your business has grown too large to run out of your home. You're going to need to _____ the bullet and rent some office space.

    a) eat   b) bite   c) take

7) Our CEO kicked _____ the company holiday party by warning people not to drink too much champagne.

    a) off   b) out   c) in

8) If you want to bring some _____ blood into the company, put an advertisement on Monster.com or another online job search site.

 a) red b) smart c) new

9) Jerry doesn't understand what's going on in the marketplace today. He's _____ touch with reality.

 a) out of b) close to c) far from

10) Don't mince _____. Tell Heather what you *really* think about her performance.

 a) words b) language c) talk

11) Irene wasn't sure she'd be able to prepare the financial reports by tomorrow's meeting, but she promised to _____ a crack at it.

 a) make b) take c) do

12) Ben pulled out all the _____ to ensure that his business partner from Chile enjoyed his visit to the United States.

 a) starts b) stops c) tricks

13) We've got a lot of employees just sitting around and playing Solitaire on their computers all day. It's time to _____ house.

 a) wash b) clean c) empty

14) If we don't roll _____ our sleeves and get started on this project, we're going to miss our deadline.

 a) down b) out c) up

15) Apple is a very innovative company. They're always dreaming _____ interesting new products.

 a) about b) up c) down

ANSWERS TO REVIEW, p. 201

I'll count on you two to rally the troops.

MOTIVATING CO-WORKERS
激勵士氣

Greg, Stan, and Donna work for Pack-It, a maker of trash bags and other consumer goods. After disappointing sales results, they discuss exiting the trash bag business. But a fresh new idea gives them hope for the future.

Greg: Our sales were down again last quarter.

Donna: We've been **working our tails off** and our results are still lousy!

Greg: Maybe we should exit the trash bag business — just **call it quits**!

Stan: C'mon.* Let's not **throw in the towel** yet. **We've been down before, but we always come back fighting**.

Donna: But this time *private-label products* are **driving us out of business**!

Stan: We've got a successful **track record**. Everybody knows that we offer quality trash bags.

Donna: That's true, but we can't just **rest on our laurels** forever.

Stan: Well, I have a new idea that's going to **turn around our business**. It's a new line of trash bags that smell like fresh fruits, such as apples and peaches.

Greg: That sounds like a great idea. I'm ready to **roll up my sleeves** and **get down to business**!

Stan: I appreciate your **team spirit**! Donna, are you **on board** too?

Donna: Sure. **Count me in.**

Stan: Great. Let's get everybody else in the company excited about this plan too. I'll count on you two to **rally the troops.**

* c'mon – This casual expression is short for "come on" and here means "listen to me."

IDIOMS & EXPRESSIONS - LESSON 11

(to) work one's tail off   賣力工作
to work very hard

EXAMPLE: The software developers **worked their tails off** to get the new software package released before Christmas.

(to) call it quits   放棄／認輸
to give up; to quit; to stop; to admit defeat

EXAMPLE: When Borders announced they were building a new bookstore in town, the small book shop decided to **call it quits.**

(to) throw in the towel   投降／放棄
to give up; to surrender; to admit defeat

EXAMPLE: After several years of trying to run a small business from his home, Patrick finally decided to **throw in the towel.**

ORIGIN: This idiom comes from boxing. When a fighter was losing a match, his assistant would toss a towel into the ring to signal defeat and end the game. That towel was the same one used to wipe the sweat and blood off the boxer's face.

We've been down before, but we always come back fighting.
我們有過低潮，但每次都能捲土重來。
everything is going to be okay; we've had trouble in the past too, and we managed to get over that

EXAMPLE: We need to be optimistic about our future. **We've been down before, but we always come back fighting.**

track record　績效紀錄
a record of achievement or performances

EXAMPLE: General Electric has a proven **track record** of making successful acquisitions.

(to) rest on one's laurels　靠過去功績／活在過去的成功裡
to believe that past success is enough to guarantee that the future will also be successful; to rely too much on reputation

EXAMPLE: The CEO made several positive changes during his first two years with the company, but now people say he's just **resting on his laurels**.

ORIGIN: In Ancient Roman times, a crown made of laurels (from the laurel tree) was a symbol of victory.

(to) turn around one's business　轉虧為盈
to make a business profitable again; to go from not making profits to being profitable again

EXAMPLE: The telecom company was able to **turn around its business** by developing a popular new line of services.

(to) roll up one's sleeves
see Lesson 10

(to) get down to business　進入正題／開始談正事
to start work; to begin discussing the important issues

EXAMPLE: We could talk about last night's baseball game for hours, but let's **get down to business** and start the negotiation.

team spirit　團隊精神
enthusiasm; enthusiasm about doing something for the group

EXAMPLE: Jill is always organizing company trips and lunches. She's got a lot of **team spirit**.

on board 贊同／支持
ready to participate; in agreement

EXAMPLE: Before we agree to sign this contract with our new partner, we'd better make sure our president is **on board**.

....

count me in 算我一份／我也加入
I will participate

EXAMPLE: You're organizing a farewell party for Christine? **Count me in**.

NOTE: You may also hear the shorter variation of this expression: I'm in. Example: You're organizing a farewell party for Christine? **I'm in**.

....

(to) rally the troops 激勵士氣
to motivate others; to get other people excited about doing something; to do something to improve the morale of the employees and get them energized about doing their work

EXAMPLE: After the lay-offs and salary cuts, the airline president organized a meeting to **rally the troops** and plan for the next year.

NOTE: The verb "to rally" has several definitions, but in this case means to "call together for a common goal or purpose." Troops is an informal way of describing a group of employees. The term comes from the military — a troop is a military unit.

✎ PRACTICE THE IDIOMS

Fill in the blanks using the following idioms:

track record	on board
count me in	team spirit
rally the troops	turn around our business
throw in the towel	working their tails off

Kim: Sales at our Westport furniture store are down by 50 percent this year. I've got a plan to _____(1)_____. For the month of December, we'll stand on street corners with big signs advertising our store.

Jason: Stand on street corners in this cold weather? Maybe we should just _____(2)_____ and close the Westport store. Our other five stores are still doing well.

Cindy: Kim, I like your idea. I'm ready to participate. _____(3)_____!

Mark: I'm _____(4)_____ too.

Cindy: I'd be happy to _____(5)_____ and get all of our other employees to join us, starting with Jason.

Kim: Yeah, Jason. Where's your _____(6)_____? Everybody else is going to participate.

Mark: Right, Jason. You're going to feel guilty when everybody else is _____(7)_____ outside while you're inside drinking coffee and relaxing.

Jason: Okay, I'll do it. I just can't believe that with our excellent _____(8)_____ , we now have to take such desperate action!

ANSWERS TO LESSON 11, p. 201

Let's get down to business.

RUNNING A MEETING
主持會議

Julia is running a meeting. When Larry and Sally start arguing, Julia has to bring the meeting back under control.

Julia: Let's **get down to business**. We need to **cover a lot of ground**. Our first *agenda item* is to figure out how we're going to respond to all the complaints we've been getting about our new website.

Larry: Just so we're all **on the same page**, please give us an *overview* of the problem.

Julia: **In a nutshell**, our customers are complaining that it's very difficult to place orders through the new website.

Sally: I think we **jumped the gun** by not conducting *focus groups* with our customers before we *launched our new website*.

Larry: More focus groups? **Every time I turn around** we're running focus groups! It's **gotten out of hand**.

Sally: **I beg to differ**. Focus groups are very important. They help us better understand our customer.

Julia: Well, clearly you two don't **see eye to eye** on this issue.

Larry: Ha! **That's putting it lightly**! Focus groups are a waste of time and they…

Julia: Excuse me, let's not **get off track** here. Does anybody else want to **weigh in on the issue at hand**?

Carl: If I can **put in my two cents**, I agree with Sally that focus groups would've been a good idea.

Julia: Well, enough about focus groups for now. Let's **move on** to our next *agenda item* — planning for our *company offsite*.

Larry: Wait, I'm not finished talking about the website!

Julia: We can **circle back to** that at the end of our meeting if we have time. I want to keep us on schedule since I know many of us have another meeting at 11 o'clock.

IDIOMS & EXPRESSIONS - LESSON 12

(to) get down to business
see Lesson 11

....

(to) cover a lot of ground 有許多議程／談到很多問題
to discuss many topics; to have a productive discussion

EXAMPLE: That was an excellent meeting. We **covered a lot of ground**.

....

(to be) on the same page
see Lesson 5

....

in a nutshell 簡而言之
in summary; in short

EXAMPLE: I won't go into the details now. **In a nutshell**, our sales are down 50 percent versus one year ago.

....

(to) jump the gun 進行得太快、太倉促
to start doing something too soon or ahead of everybody else

EXAMPLE: The company **jumped the gun** by releasing a new product before the results of the consumer testing were in.

ORIGIN: A runner "jumps the gun" if he or she starts running before the starter's pistol has been fired.

every time I turn around 一天到晚
frequently; too often

EXAMPLE: **Every time I turn around**, Lisa is checking her stock portfolio on Yahoo. No wonder she never gets any work done.

(to be or to get) out of hand 多得離譜
to be too much; to be out of control

EXAMPLE: Ed has called in sick 10 times this month. The situation is **getting out of hand**.

I beg to differ 我持不同意見
I don't agree (a formal way of telling somebody you don't agree with them)

EXAMPLE: You think Tim has the leadership skills required to run this division? **I beg to differ!**

(to) see eye to eye 意見相同
to be in agreement; to have the same opinion

EXAMPLE: Our manufacturing and our marketing people fight with each other all the time. They don't **see eye to eye** on anything.

that's putting it lightly 再正確不過了
that's definitely true; that's for sure; that's an understatement

EXAMPLE: "You were upset when your husband lost his job?" — "**That's putting it lightly!**"

(to) get off track 離題
to get off the subject; to lose focus; to digress

EXAMPLE: We've **gotten off track**. This meeting was supposed to be about our new sales strategy, but we ended up talking about Erin's vacation in Spain!

(to) weigh in on 表達意見
to say something about; to comment on; to express an opinion

EXAMPLE: We'd like you to **weigh in on** some ideas we have for new products.

the issue at hand 現在討論的議題

the topic under discussion; what's being talked about now

EXAMPLE: We've somehow gotten off the topic. Let's return to **the issue at hand**.

....

(to) put in one's two cents 發表個人意見

to offer one's opinion; to give an opinion without being asked

EXAMPLE: Let me just **put in my two cents** and say that I think we should definitely move our manufacturing to China.

....

(to) move on

1) 進行 *to proceed*

EXAMPLE: It's time we **move on** to our next topic.

2) （離開舊工作）從事新工作 *to leave a job and do something else*

EXAMPLE: Don't feel too bad that you were fired. It was probably time for you to **move on** anyway.

....

(to) circle back to 回到⋯⋯

to return to

EXAMPLE: I'd like to **circle back** to something Maria said earlier in the meeting.

✍ PRACTICE THE IDIOMS

Choose the best substitute for the phrase or sentence in bold:

1) Jim thinks his company should outsource its customer service to India, but his boss thinks they should keep it in California. **They don't see eye to eye on the issue.**
   a) They don't understand the issue.
   b) They don't agree on the issue.
   c) They agree on the issue.

2) We're going to conduct focus groups so consumers can **weigh in on** the design of some of our new products.
   a) complain about
   b) dictate
   c) give their opinion on

3) I know we're in a hurry to end the meeting, but let me just **circle back to** something David said earlier.
   a) emphasize
   b) return to
   c) dismiss

4) **Every time I turn around**, Ellen and Kelly are chatting.
   a) very frequently
   b) whenever I turn my back
   c) from time to time

5) **Let's not jump the gun** by buying a new printer before we can see if the old one can be fixed.
   a) let's not act too quickly
   b) let's take action now
   c) let's be efficient

6) I know many of you have more to say on this issue, but I'm afraid we're going to have to **move on** so we can finish this meeting on time.
   a) continue to discuss this
   b) leave the conference room now
   c) proceed to our next topic

7) Our office expenses are **out of hand**. We're going to have to stop spending so much.
   a) hard to count
   b) written down
   c) much too high

8) Calvin **covered a lot of ground** with his local partners during his business trip to Tokyo.
   a) saw much of the city
   b) had successful conversations
   c) made a lot of money

ANSWERS TO LESSON 12, p. 201

When filling out order forms, you need to dot your i's and cross your t's.

DISCUSSING A MISTAKE
討論業務疏失

Chris and Todd work for Alpine Design, a furniture manufacturer. When Todd accidentally orders the wrong amount of wood, his boss, Chris, warns him to be more careful in the future.

Chris: Todd, we got our shipment of wood yesterday. We're *short by* 18 tons.

Todd: Our wood supplier must've made a mistake. **I could've sworn that** I ordered the right amount.

Chris: You'd better go back and *double-check* your order.

Todd: Oops, you're right. I accidentally ordered two tons instead of twenty. **No big deal**. I'll just put in another order.

Chris: When filling out order forms, you need to **dot your i's and cross your t's**. You shouldn't be making careless mistakes like this.

Todd: I just forgot to add a zero after the two. Don't **make a mountain out of a molehill**. No need to **blow things out of proportion**.

Chris: This is very serious. Now we won't have enough wood to finish the furniture order we got from La-Z Boy.

Todd: Okay, sorry I **dropped the ball**.

Chris: Todd, this may be a **bitter pill to swallow**, but your work lately hasn't been **up to scratch**. You've really been **asleep at the wheel**!

I could've sworn that... 我發誓……
I really thought that; I was convinced that

EXAMPLE: You didn't know we already hired somebody for the sales director position? **I could've sworn that** I told you.

NOTE: "Sworn" is the past perfect tense of "swear."

---

no big deal 沒什麼大不了
it's not a problem

EXAMPLE: Our coffee machine broke? **No big deal**. Our employees will just have to go to Starbucks until we get a new one.

(to) dot your i's and cross your t's 格外留意細節
to be very careful; to pay attention to details

EXAMPLE: When preparing financial statements, accuracy is very important. Be sure to **dot your i's and cross your t's**.

(to) make a mountain out of a molehill 小題大作／大驚小怪
to make a big deal out of something small or insignificant

EXAMPLE: Don't be angry at your boss for not complimenting you on your presentation. He probably just forgot. Don't **make a mountain out of a molehill**.

(to) blow things out of proportion 小題大作
to exaggerate; to make more of something than one should

EXAMPLE: Our CEO says that if we don't meet our sales target for the month, our company is going to go out of business. He's probably **blowing things out of proportion**.

(to) drop the ball 搞砸了
to make a mistake; to fail; to do something poorly

EXAMPLE: You forgot to submit the budget? You really **dropped the ball**!

ORIGIN: When a football player drops the ball, his team may lose the chance to score.

bitter pill to swallow 刺耳的話

bad news; something unpleasant to accept

EXAMPLE: After Gina spent her whole summer working as an intern for American Express, failing to get a full-time job offer from the company was a **bitter pill to swallow**.

up to scratch 達到水準

good; at the expected level

EXAMPLE: Your customer service call center isn't **up to scratch**. They put me on hold for 45 minutes!

NOTE: You will usually hear this expression in the negative: not up to scratch.

asleep at the wheel 怠忽職守

not performing well; neglecting responsibilities; not paying attention to what's going on

EXAMPLE: The dental hygienist was **asleep at the wheel**. She accidentally left a big piece of dental floss in the patient's mouth!

SYNONYM: asleep at the switch; out to lunch

✒ PRACTICE THE IDIOMS

Fill in the blanks using the following idioms:

up to scratch	dot your i's and cross your t's
asleep at the wheel	no big deal
bitter pill to swallow	I could've sworn that
drop the ball	blow things out of proportion

Ryan: Eric, we got fifty phone calls this week complaining that our spicy nacho chips are much too spicy. Do you have the machine set correctly?

Eric: Let me check…No, we've got the machine set wrong. It's putting in three times too much hot pepper. That's strange. _____(1)_____ I checked it this morning and it was okay.

Ryan: Oh, for heaven's sake! How could you _____(2)_____ like this? You must be _____(3)_____.

Eric: Ryan, please don't _____(4)_____. It's really _____(5)_____. I'll just turn this knob right now and adjust the setting.

Ryan: In the future, please be sure to _____(6)_____.

Eric: No need to make a mountain out of a molehill. It's just one little mistake. Some people prefer extra spicy nacho chips anyway!

Ryan: It's not just one little mistake. Lately, your work hasn't been _____(7)_____. This may be a _____(8)_____, but several of us have noticed that your performance has been poor for the past six months.

ANSWERS TO LESSON 13, p. 201

TAKING CREDIT FOR GOOD RESULTS
討論大家的功勞

When United Supply Company launches their website three weeks ahead of schedule, there's more than one person ready to take credit.

Bob: Kurt, I've got great news for you. We're **pushing the envelope** and *launching our new website* three weeks ahead of schedule.

Kurt: Wow, Bob, that's a first for this company! How did you **pull that off**?

Bob: I **burned the midnight oil** over these past few weeks. I **worked my tail off**. Sometimes things would get *tough*, but I always **kept my eye on the prize**.

Tara: Let's not forget about Jim in technical support. He really **hunkered down** these past few days, working **around the clock**.

Bob: Yeah, Jim's a real **team player.** He helped a lot.

Kurt: Well, that's not surprising. Jim's always ready to **pitch in**.

Bob: Of course, you deserve **a pat on the back** too, Kurt. None of this would've been possible without your leadership.

Kurt: **All in a day's work**. Providing great leadership **comes with the territory**. Well, time for some **R&R**. I'm off to Florida to play golf for a few days. See you next week!

(to) push the envelope 超越一般水準

to go beyond what is normally done; to stretch the boundaries

EXAMPLE: The design team **pushed the envelope** by creating a car powered entirely by the sun.

(to) pull something off 完成艱鉅的任務

to accomplish a difficult task; to successfully do something difficult

EXAMPLE: We need to prepare and mail out 50,000 media kits by tomorrow. I don't know how we're going to **pull it off**!

SYNONYM: to carry something off

(to) burn the midnight oil 焚膏繼晷

to stay up late working or studying

EXAMPLE: The bank needs our financial statements completed by 9 a.m. tomorrow. We're going to need to **burn the midnight oil** tonight to finish on time.

ORIGIN: This expression dates back to the days before electricity, when oil lamps were used for lighting. People went to sleep earlier back then, so if you were still burning the oil at midnight, you were staying up late.

(to work one's tail off

see Lesson 11

(to) keep one's eye on the prize 專注於目標

to stay focused on the end result; to not let small problems get in the way of good results

EXAMPLE: I know it's difficult going to class after work, but just **keep your eye on the prize**. At the end of next year, you'll have your MBA.

NOTE: You will also see the variation: keep one's eyes on the prize.

(to) hunker down 賣力工作
to focus on work; to get ready to work hard, often involving a long period of time

EXAMPLE: If you're going to finish that report by Monday morning, you'd better **hunker down** over the weekend.

NOTE: This phrase also means to stay indoors or to take shelter when the weather turns bad. Example: There's going to be a blizzard tonight. We'd better just **hunker down**.

....

around the clock 不眠不休
non-stop; 24 hours a day

EXAMPLE: When the company website went down, the IT department worked **around the clock** to fix it.

NOTE: You may also hear the variation: round the clock.

....

team player 有團隊精神的人
somebody willing to help out for the benefit of the group

EXAMPLE: Aaron is great at working with others, and he always contributes a lot to projects. Everybody knows he's a **team player**!

....

(to) pitch in 幫忙／效力
to help; to contribute

EXAMPLE: If we're going to get these 3,000 crystal vases packaged and shipped by tomorrow morning, everybody's going to need to **pitch in**.

....

a pat on the back
see Lesson 6

....

all in a day's work 不足掛齒／應該的
this is just part of the job; this is nothing unusual

EXAMPLE: "You've come up with a plan to double our sales next quarter?" — "Yes, **all in a day's work**."

(to) come with the territory 工作的一部分
to be part of the job

EXAMPLE: Samantha doesn't like firing people, but as a vice president, she knows that **comes with the territory**.

⋯⋯⋯⋯⋯⋯⋯⋯⋯⋯⋯⋯⋯⋯⋯⋯⋯⋯⋯⋯⋯⋯⋯⋯

R&R 休息放鬆
rest and relaxation

EXAMPLE: Brad and Melanie got plenty of **R&R** during their two-week vacation in the Caribbean.

✎ PRACTICE THE IDIOMS

Choose the best substitute for the phrase or sentence in bold:

1) Your small company is trying to get distribution at Wal-Mart? How are you going to **pull that off?**
   a) succeed in doing that
   b) fail to do that
   c) compete with them

2) If you need help answering phones and taking orders, I'd be happy to **pitch in**.
   a) hang up on the customers
   b) help
   c) call

3) When you're the CEO of a tobacco company, dealing with lawsuits **comes with the territory**.
   a) is a great benefit
   b) is easily avoided
   c) is part of the job

4) If we're going to get all of these orders shipped in time for Christmas, we're going to have to **hunker down**!
   a) close for the holidays
   b) work really hard
   c) take it easy

5) During the negotiation, **keep your eye on the prize** and don't let the other side pressure you into a bad deal.
   a) watch the prize carefully
   b) stay focused on what's really important
   c) grab everything for yourself

6) You think consumers will be willing to pay $50,000 for a high-tech toilet? That's **pushing the envelope.**
   a) testing the limits of what people will pay
   b) a very reasonable price
   c) not something to be flushed down a toilet

7) You look exhausted. Why don't you take a few days off and **get some R&R**?
   a) spend some time relaxing
   b) take a trip by train
   c) work extra hours

8) If we want to submit the business plan by tomorrow afternoon, we're going to have to **burn the midnight oil** tonight.
   a) work until 7 p.m.
   b) relax
   c) work very late

ANSWERS TO LESSON 14, p. 201

Stop trying to pass the buck.

SHIFTING BLAME
推卸責任

Rick and Ellen work for Attic Treasures Antiques, an antique shop. Max is the owner of the shop. Recently, a woman came in and sold them $10,000 worth of "antique" jewelry. Max takes one look at the jewelry and realizes it's fake.

Max: I can't believe you two bought these fake antique necklaces! Didn't you examine them before **shelling out** 10 *grand?*

Rick: Yeah, I thought they were fake, but I let Ellen **talk me into** buying them.

Ellen: What? **I can't believe my ears**! You thought they were real. Now you're just trying to **cover yourself**!

Rick: I don't want to be the **fall guy** here, Ellen. You were the one who looked at them under a magnifying glass.

Ellen: **For the record**, you were the one **going on about** how you "**struck gold**" right after the woman left the shop!

Rick: I don't remember saying that. Stop trying to **pass the buck**. Just **step up to the plate** and admit your mistake!

Ellen: Right, while you **wash your hands of** the whole thing. **Dream on!**

Max: Let's stop **pointing fingers at each other**. We need to **track down that woman** and get the money back!

(to) shell out　灑錢

to pay (often more than one would like)

EXAMPLE: The fast food chain had to **shell out** $10 million in a lawsuit after several people got sick from eating their hamburgers.

(to) talk someone into something　說服某人

to convince someone to do something, often something that one later regrets

EXAMPLE: Our president doesn't want to give us Christmas Eve off as a holiday. We're hoping our office manager can **talk him into** it.

I can't believe my ears!　你說什麼？我真不敢相信
I'm very surprised!

EXAMPLE: Chris got fired? **I can't believe my ears!** He was one of our top salespeople!

(to) cover oneself　推卸責任以自保

to try to avoid being blamed for something; to protect oneself from blame

EXAMPLE: Nina knew her company was producing a defective product. She **covered herself** by keeping records of all of her letters and e-mails to her boss about the issue.

NOTE: You may hear the more vulgar form of this expression: cover your ass, or the shortened version "CYA." Since "ass" is a vulgar word, some people use more polite variations of this expression, such as "cover your behind" and "cover your butt."

fall guy　替罪羔羊
the person who gets blamed for a mistake, sometimes unfairly

EXAMPLE: The company's entire management team wanted to enter the market in China. When the business failed there, they made Fred the **fall guy** and fired him.

for the record
see Lesson 4

(to) go on about　滔滔不絕
to talk too long about; to talk for a long time about (always said as a criticism); to brag

EXAMPLE: Bill is always **going on about** what a great salesman he is.

(to) strike gold　挖到寶
to make a very profitable deal; to discover something valuable

EXAMPLE: Christie **struck gold** with the idea of selling videos at discount prices on eBay.

(to) pass the buck　踢皮球／卸責給他人
to shift the blame; to blame somebody else

EXAMPLE: It's your fault. Don't try to **pass the buck**!

ORIGIN: This expression comes from the world of poker. In the nineteenth century, a knife with a buckhorn handle (the "buck") was passed to the next dealer when it was his turn to give out the cards.

(to) step up to the plate
see Lesson 4

(to) wash one's hands of　脫身／自清
to remove any association with; to stop being part of something; to refuse to take responsibility for

EXAMPLE: When Molly realized her business partners were selling stolen goods, she decided to **wash her hands** of the whole business.

ORIGIN: This expression comes from the Bible. Pontius Pilate, a Roman official, announced before a crowd that he wouldn't save Jesus from execution. Then he washed his hands in front of the crowd, symbolically washing away the responsibility.

Dream on! 作夢吧！想都別想
That's what you'd like, but it's not realistic.

EXAMPLE: You want to retire in five years, and you've only got $5,000 in the bank? **Dream on!**

....

(to) point fingers at each other / (to) point the finger at some-one 互相攻訐
to blame

EXAMPLE: Don't **point the finger at me**! You need to take the blame for this mistake.

....

(to) track something down 追討…
to find, usually with difficulty

EXAMPLE: Sheila left an important file in a taxi, and now she's going to have to **track it down**.

✎ PRACTICE THE IDIOMS

Choose the most appropriate response to the following:

1) Please don't try to talk me into exhibiting at your trade show this year.
   a) Okay, I'll sign you up.
   b) Okay, I'll call you tomorrow to talk about it some more.
   c) Okay, if you're sure you're not interested, I won't ask again.

2) I can't find Sam's address anywhere. Do you think you can help me track it down?
   a) Yes, I'd be happy to track it.
   b) Sure, I'll help you find it.
   c) No, but I'll help you find it.

3) We've already shelled out enough on advertising this year.
    a) I agree. Let's spend more.
    b) I know we've spent a lot, but I think we should do a couple more radio ads.
    c) I disagree. We've already spent a lot of money on advertising.

4) You think you'll be accepted to Harvard Business School? Dream on!
    a) You may not agree, but I think it's a realistic goal.
    b) Right, I'll just go to sleep and dream about it.
    c) Thanks for helping me think big.

5) I had nothing to do with the disastrous decision to hire Dennis. Don't point the finger at me!
    a) I'm not pointing the finger, but I *am* blaming you.
    b) Good. I'm glad you're willing to take the blame.
    c) Okay, I won't blame you.

6) I think we've struck gold with our idea to sell content on our website instead of giving it away for free. What do you think?
    a) I agree. It's a great idea.
    b) I agree. Nobody's going to be willing to pay for it.
    c) I agree. We should sell silver and bronze on the site too.

7) You need to take responsibility for our accounting problems. Stop trying to pass the buck!
    a) Okay, I won't pass it anymore. You can have it.
    b) I already passed the buck.
    c) I'm not trying to pass the buck. I admit I made a mistake.

8) You finally got promoted, and now you're leaving your company and opening a health food store? I can't believe my ears!
    a) Yes, I know it's a surprising move.
    b) I couldn't believe my ears either.
    c) I know you're not surprised.

ANSWERS TO LESSON 15, p. 201

REVIEW FOR LESSONS 11-15

Fill in the blank with the missing word:

1) Walter has an opinion about everything. No matter what the topic is, he has to put in his _____ cents.

   a) ten   b) five   c) two

2) I can't believe that Katrina forgot to order sandwiches for our lunch meeting. She really _____ the ball!

   a) left   b) dropped   c) forgot

3) Sales are down by 30 percent so far this year. Let's think of some ways we can turn _____ the business.

   a) up   b) about   c) around

4) Our copy machine is broken. Before we shell _____ for a new one, let's call the repairman and see if he can fix it.

   a) out   b) up   c) about

5) The pharmaceutical company spent millions of dollars trying to come up with a cure for cancer, before finally deciding to throw _____ the towel.

   a) out   b) up   c) in

6) I won't go over all the details in the contract with you now, but _____ a nutshell, we are offering to pay you $150,000 a year for your services.

   a) by   b) in   c) with

7) Joan's letters to clients often have typos in them. In the future, she should _____ her i's and _____ her t's.

   a) cross...dot   b) dot...cross   c) label...watch

8) We're going to _____ the envelope and try a brand new type of online advertising this year.

   a) push   b) pull   c) address

9) One of our customers is looking for a humidifier that also works as an air filter. Can you help her track that _____?
   a) down   b) up   c) out

10) You need to speak with Brandon about his performance. Lately, it hasn't been _____ to scratch.

   a) down   b) about   c) up

11) Since he made the big sale two years ago, Mike hasn't worked very hard. He's been _____ on his laurels.

   a) resting   b) sleeping   c) relying

12) Before we make a final decision, does anybody else want to weigh _____ on this issue?

   a) out   b) in   c) about

13) Don't try to pass the _____ to your employees. It's time you take some responsibility.

   a) buck   b) dollar   c) responsibility

14) We've got to call 200 customers as part of our market research survey. Who's going to pitch _____ and start making calls?

   a) out   b) up   c) in

15) If we get _____ track, we're not going to be able to finish our meeting on time.

   a) on   b) around   c) off

ANSWERS TO REVIEW, p. 202

We need to do some belt-tightening.

POLITELY DISAGREEING
WITH SOMEONE
客客氣氣地表達異議

If Kroll Enterprises doesn't take action soon, the company is going to be in financial trouble. Joel and Kathy have different opinions on how to cut costs at the company.

Kathy: We're going to be **in the red** again this year.

Joel: I think we should **cut back on** employee health benefits. We could **save a bundle**.

Kathy: True, it might help the **bottom line**, but our employees would be really unhappy. I would only recommend it as a **last resort**.

Joel: Well, we need to do some **belt-tightening**. We can either have a *salary freeze* or we can cut back on the health benefits. I think I've chosen **the lesser of two evils**.

Kathy: Another *salary freeze* is **out of the question**. All our best employees will quit.

Joel: I'm caught **between a rock and a hard place**. I have to cut costs.

Kathy: Do you really? I don't think cutting costs is **the name of the game**. I think the secret is figuring out how to increase our sales.

Joel: How do you suggest we **pull that off**?

Kathy: Let's meet with the other vice presidents and **bat around some ideas**.

Joel: We can talk **until we're blue in the face**. We need to take action now.

Kathy: It's clear that you and I don't **see eye to eye**. For now, **let's just agree to disagree**.

IDIOMS & EXPRESSIONS - LESSON 16

in the red – see Lesson 2

(to) cut back on 刪減
to reduce

EXAMPLE: We need to save money by **cutting back on** business travel. Please conduct most of your meetings by videoconference from now on.

(to) save a bundle 省下一大筆錢
to save a lot of money

EXAMPLE: By outsourcing their call center operations to India, the credit card company **saved a bundle**.

bottom line
1) 利潤 *profits; financial results*

EXAMPLE: Falling prices for televisions and other electronic equipment have hurt Sony's **bottom line**.

2) 重點 *the final result; the main point*

EXAMPLE: The **bottom line** is that your company is not big enough to supply us with all of the packaging we need.

NOTE: In accounting, the bottom line (the last line) of the income statement shows net income (the profit after deducting all expenses). This is one of the most important numbers for a company.

last resort　最後手段
if there are no other alternatives left; the last solution for getting out of a difficulty

EXAMPLE: There must be some way to create more demand for our products. We should only lower our prices as a **last resort**.

....

belt-tightening　減少開銷
reduction of expenses

EXAMPLE: When worldwide demand for software decreased, Microsoft had to do some **belt-tightening**.

....

the lesser of two evils　必要之惡／二害相權取其輕也
when you have two unattractive options and you choose the one that is better; the better of two bad options

EXAMPLE: Both shuttle services offering rides to the airport are bad. You'll just have to choose **the lesser of two evils**.

....

out of the question　不可能
impossible

EXAMPLE: We couldn't possibly afford to open an office in Europe right now. It's **out of the question**.

....

between a rock and a hard place　陷入兩難
in a very difficult position; facing two choices which are equally unacceptable or difficult

EXAMPLE: I wish I could offer you a better discount, but my boss would be angry. I'm caught **between a rock and a hard place**.

....

the name of the game　關鍵／重點
the central issue; the most important thing; the main goal

EXAMPLE: If we're going to operate more effectively, better communication is **the name of the game**.

....

(to) pull something off
see Lesson 14

(to) bat around some ideas   討論方法、解決之道
to discuss ideas; to discuss options

EXAMPLE: We need to come up with a creative marketing plan. Let's meet on Monday morning to **bat around some ideas**.

until one is blue in the face   談到天都黑了還是毫無進展
for a very long time, with no results

EXAMPLE: You can argue with the customer service people **until you're blue in the face**, but they won't give you your money back.

(to) see eye to eye
see Lesson 12

let's just agree to disagree   包容歧異
we don't agree, but let's not argue further; let's accept our differences of opinion and move on

EXAMPLE: I don't want to get in a fight with you about this. **Let's just agree to disagree**.

✎ PRACTICE THE IDIOMS

Choose the best substitute for the phrase or sentence in bold:

1) I know we need to **do some belt-tightening**, but I'm not sure that laying off employees is the solution.
   a) increase our revenues
   b) get rid of some people
   c) reduce our expenses

2) Changing the packaging design at this point is **out of the question**. We're already in production.
   a) not a possibility
   b) a good idea
   c) probably not possible

3) If we're serious about saving money, we should consider **cutting back on** our use of expensive consultants.
   a) eliminating
   b) reducing
   c) increasing

4) You can tell me about how great Jim is **until you're blue in the face**. The fact is, I don't like the way he does business.
   a) until your face turns blue
   b) all you want
   c) until I change my mind

5) Kyle and Mark are meeting at Flanagan's Bar after work to **bat around some ideas about starting their own business**.
   a) discuss ideas about starting their own business
   b) dismiss the idea of starting their own business
   c) finalize plans to start their own bar

6) When you're the boss, demonstrating good leadership is **the name of the game**.
   a) not important
   b) somewhat important
   c) very important

7) The food manufacturer's costs have gone up, but they are unable to raise the price of their products. They're **caught between a rock and a hard place**.
   a) stuck in an undesirable position
   b) ready to go out of business
   c) deciding between two great options

8) Why don't you open a corporate account with DHL and ship all of your packages with them? **You could save a bundle**.
   a) You could stop carrying heavy packages.
   b) You could save a few dollars.
   c) You could save a lot of money.

ANSWERS TO LESSON 16, p. 202

Shape up or ship out!

TELLING SOMEBODY OFF* - Part 1
痛斥某人

Doug and Joe work at the reception desk of the Boston Empire Hotel, a large hotel. Kara, the hotel manager, yells at Doug for being late to work every day.

Doug: Good morning, guys. How's it going?

Joe: Lousy. You were supposed to be here at 8 a.m. It's now 11 o'clock. **What's the deal?**

Doug: Sorry about that. My alarm didn't go off this morning.

Kara: You've been late every day this week!

Doug: I **had a rough night** last night. My girlfriend Liz **dumped me** and told me she's in love with my best friend!

Kara: Oh please, **spare us the sob story**!

Joe: I'm **sick and tired of** your excuses. You need to start **pulling your weight** around here.

Doug: Hey, **cut me some slack**! My life's a mess right now.

Kara: Doug, I'm trying to **run a tight ship**. I can't continue **turning a blind eye to** the fact that you're always late. **Shape up or ship out!**

Doug: I promise tomorrow I'll be here at 8 a.m. **on the dot**.

* To "tell somebody off" （責罵） is to criticize them or yell at them for doing something wrong.

IDIOMS & EXPRESSIONS - LESSON 17
Part I

What's the deal? 發生什麼事？
What's going on? What happened? What's the explanation?

EXAMPLE: We received 5,000 mailing envelopes from your company, and you sent us an invoice for 50,000. **What's the deal?**

(to) have a rough night 晚上不太好過
to have a difficult evening or night

EXAMPLE: You look exhausted this morning. Did you **have a rough night**?

(to) dump someone 甩掉某人
to end a romantic relationship

EXAMPLE: Walter Jenkins, the CEO of a real estate firm, **dumped** his wife of 40 years and married his young assistant.

spare us *(or me)* the sob story 別找藉口了／少來
don't bother making excuses; don't try to explain yourself

EXAMPLE: You can't finish your work tonight because you've got a toothache? **Spare me the sob story**!

NOTE: "Sob" means cry.

sick and tired of 厭煩
completely bored with; sick of; fed up with

EXAMPLE: Jane is **sick and tired of** hearing her boss talk about how great he is. She's hoping to find a new job soon.

(to) pull one's weight 做好份內工作
to do one's share of the work

EXAMPLE: Don't rely on others to get your job done. You need to **pull your own weight**.

NOTE: You will also hear the variation: to pull one's own weight.

102

(to) cut someone some slack 體諒某人一點

to be forgiving; to not judge someone too harshly

EXAMPLE: **Cut Gretchen some slack** for failing to finish the report on time. She's going through a bitter divorce.

(to) run a tight ship 嚴格有效管理

to run something effectively and efficiently

EXAMPLE: Jack Welch is known as one of the greatest business leaders ever. He **ran a tight ship** while he was the CEO of General Electric.

(to) turn a blind eye to something 無視於⋯⋯／漠視

to ignore a problem or an issue; to refuse to recognize

EXAMPLE: Every September when the school year starts, pens and paper disappear from our company's supply room. We can no longer **turn a blind eye to this**.

Shape up or ship out! 限期改善，否則後果自負

improve your behavior or leave; if you don't improve your performance, you're going to get fired

EXAMPLE: Martin finally had enough of Todd's negative attitude. "**Shape up or ship out!**" he told Todd.

ORIGIN: This expression was first used in the U.S. military during World War Two, meaning: you'd better follow regulations and behave yourself ("shape up"), or you're going to be sent overseas to a war zone ("ship out").

on the dot 準時

sharp; at an exact time

EXAMPLE: The videoconference with our Tokyo office will start at 10 a.m. **on the dot**.

Doug:　Sorry, I'm **running behind**. I had to…

Kara:　**Don't waste your breath**! You're three hours late again.

Doug:　But my car wouldn't start, my mechanic is on vacation in Florida, and then I…

Kara:　Today was the **last straw**. You're fired!

Doug:　That's fine. I was miserable working for a **slave driver** like you anyway!

Kara:　**Don't burn your bridges**. You may need me later as a *reference*.

IDIOMS & EXPRESSIONS - LESSON 17
Part 2

(to be) running behind　遲到
to be late; to be delayed

EXAMPLE: I'm calling to say I'm **running behind**. I'll be at your office in 15 minutes.

SYNONYM: running late

don't waste your breath　別白費唇舌
don't bother; don't bother trying to defend yourself; I don't want to hear your excuses

EXAMPLE: **Don't waste your breath** trying to talk me into buying an advertisement in your magazine. I've already spent my advertising budget for the year.

(the) last straw　令人忍無可忍的行為
the final offense or annoyance that pushes one to take action

EXAMPLE: First you tell me I can't have an office and now you're cutting my salary. This is **the last straw**. I quit!

ORIGIN: This saying comes from another expression that you may also hear: the straw that broke the camel's back. When you load up a camel straw by straw, each individual straw doesn't weigh much. However, eventually, the load will get so heavy that one extra straw will break the camel's back. In the same way, people can tolerate small annoyances. But when there get to be too many, people finally get fed up and take action.

slave driver　奴隸監工（引申為苛刻的老闆）
a very demanding and often cruel boss or supervisor

EXAMPLE: You're going to be working late hours as an assistant brand manager in Linda's group. She's a real **slave driver**!

ORIGIN: In the days of slavery, the slave driver was the person who oversaw the slaves as they worked.

(to) burn one's bridges　別把話說絕／別撕破臉
to do something which makes it impossible to go back; to damage a relationship to such an extent that one can never go back to that person again

EXAMPLE: When he was fired, Chad really felt like telling Lisa that she was a terrible manager, but he didn't want to **burn his bridges**.

ORIGIN: This expression comes from the military. Soldiers dating back to the days of the Roman Empire used to burn the bridges behind them. This meant the Roman troops couldn't retreat; they had to keep moving forward. It also made it more difficult for the enemy to follow them.

✎ PRACTICE THE IDIOMS

Fill in the blanks, using the following idioms.

slave driver	the last straw
shape up or ship out	run a tight ship
turn a blind eye	What's the deal?
cut me some slack	pulling his weight
sick and tired	spare me the sob story

Jill is a manager of the automotive department at Sears. One of her salespeople,

Len, isn't _____(1)_____. Jill is _____(2)_____ of the fact that Len shows up

late every day and is constantly flirting with Tatiana, the saleswoman in the

electronics department. Yesterday, Jill watched as Len was rude to a customer.

"Go get your tires somewhere else!" Len yelled at the customer. That was

_____(3)_____. She pulled him aside and said to him, "Len, _____(4)_____!"

Len was surprised. "_____5)_____" he asked. "I thought you and I were friends,

and now suddenly you're turning into a _____(6)_____." Jill replied, "Len, I do

like you, but I'm trying to _____(7)_____ here. I can no longer _____(8)_____

to the fact that you're not taking this job very seriously." Len turned red and

frowned. "Hey, _____(9)_____. I've been under a lot of stress lately at home."

Jill didn't want to hear any excuses. "_____(10)_____," she replied.

ANSWERS TO LESSON 17, p. 202

DISCUSSING OFFICE SCANDALS
討論辦公室八卦

With his naughty behavior, Bill Swing provides plenty of material for office gossip. Cindy and Steve discuss his latest move and review his other recent insensitive behavior.

Cindy: Did you hear **the latest dirt**?

Steve: Of course not. I'm totally **out of the loop**! I'm always the last one to find out everything.

Cindy: **According to the rumor mill**, Bill Swing **made a pass at** Laura Teller, the new marketing manager. Now she's threatening to sue him for *sexual harassment.*

Steve: Sounds like Bill's **up to his old tricks** again. He's always **on the make**. Last year, Paula Reynolds accused him of pinching her...

Cindy: I remember that. Too bad Paula quit before they could **get to the bottom of it**.

Steve: Two years ago he **got nailed** for organizing a *company offsite* to a *strip joint!*

Cindy: Oh, that really **takes the cake**. That's so **un-PC**!

Steve: Bill is definitely *not* **politically correct**!

Cindy: **What goes around comes around**. One day, **he'll get his**.

the latest dirt 最新的八卦
the latest gossip

EXAMPLE: Have you heard **the latest dirt**? Rob was fired for calling the chairman of the board a "jerk" to his face.

out of the loop 消息不靈通
unaware of what's going on

EXAMPLE: If you want to know what's really going on at the company, don't bother asking Adam. He's **out of the loop**.

according to the rumor mill 據謠傳
according to gossip

EXAMPLE: **According to the rumor mill**, Neil didn't leave his position voluntarily. He was fired.

(to) make a pass at someone 挑逗／非禮
to make a sexual advance toward someone

EXAMPLE: Glen got drunk at the office holiday party and **made a pass at** Amber, his secretary. Unfortunately for Glen, Amber's boyfriend was in the same room!

up to one's old tricks 又在玩老把戲
repeating the same behavior as before (usually annoying, dishonest, or sneaky behavior)

EXAMPLE: Our boss is **up to his old tricks**. This is the third time we've gone out to lunch and he's forgotten his wallet back at the office.

on the make
This idiom has 2 very different meanings:
1) 物色性伴侶、床伴 *actively looking for a sexual partner*

EXAMPLE: Look at Ron flirting with our new receptionist! He's always **on the make**.

2) 爭逐名利／急於晉升　*aggressively trying to improve one's social or financial status*

EXAMPLE: Jeff works 80-hour weeks as an investment banker in Manhattan. He's as an ambitious young man **on the make**.

get to the bottom of something
see Lesson 7

(to) get nailed　被抓包了
to get in trouble; to get caught doing something

EXAMPLE: Troy tried to cheat on his expense report by including a dinner he had with his girlfriend, but he **got nailed** and had to return the money.

(to) take the cake　最經典的例子
to rank first; to be the best or worst example of something

EXAMPLE: Stuart stole your idea and presented it as his own during the meeting? That really **takes the cake**!

ORIGIN: Dating back to Ancient Greek times, a cake was a popular prize given to contest winners.

un-PC　沒水準、冒犯人的／非政治正確的
insensitive; offensive; not politically correct (PC)

EXAMPLE: George came right out and asked his colleague if he was gay? That's so **un-PC**!

politically correct (PC)　政治正確的／合時宜的
This expression refers to language or behavior that is carefully controlled (sometimes too controlled) to avoid offending people based on gender, ethnicity, etc. The concept emerged in the 1980's in the United States. Nowadays, it often has a negative meaning.

EXAMPLE: The university president suggested that women may not be as good as men in science because of differences in their brains. That's not **politically correct**!

what goes around comes around　種什麼因，得什麼果
people usually get what they deserve in the end

EXAMPLE: Dana is always trying to steal everybody else's clients. But **what goes around comes around**.

....

he'll get his / she'll get hers　惡有惡報
something bad will happen to him (or her), just as he (or she) deserves

EXAMPLE: Cheryl got promoted to vice president after firing half her staff? Don't worry, **she'll get hers**.

SYNONYM: he (or she) will get what's coming to him (or her)

✒ PRACTICE THE IDIOMS

Choose the best substitute for the phrase or sentence in bold:

1) Jake says he only hires pretty girls to work at his restaurant. He's so **un-PC!**
   a) bad with computers
   b) kind
   c) offensive

2) Tiffany called in sick on Tuesday, and she showed up for work on Wednesday with a suntan. She's going to **get nailed** for lying about being sick.
   a) be awarded
   b) get in trouble
   c) get fired

3) Brad said that Tammy **made a pass at him** while they were on a business trip in Moscow.
   a) tried to initiate a sexual relationship with him
   b) threw a football at him
   c) was rude to him

4) Frank keeps taking all of the best customer accounts for himself. We hope that one of these days, **he'll get his**.
   a) he'll get his own accounts
   b) something bad will happen to him
   c) he'll actually earn the accounts he's taking

5) I'm not surprised that Randy kept trying to put his arm around you during the business dinner. He's always **on the make**.
   a) affectionate in public
   b) looking for romance
   c) moving quickly

6) Our CEO was one of the last people to hear of the accounting scandal at our company. He's so **out of the loop!**
   a) aware of what's going on
   b) unaware of what's going on
   c) curious about what's going on

7) Monica loves to gossip, so you can always count on her for the **latest dirt**.
   a) most up-to-date gossip
   b) news of important current events
   c) nastiest rumors

8) Three months after he laid off thousands of employees on Christmas Eve, the CEO himself was fired. **What goes around comes around.**
   a) When you fire somebody, you'll probably get fired yourself soon.
   b) The CEO will still come around the offices.
   c) When people do bad things, they're usually punished in the end.

ANSWERS TO LESSON 18, p. 202

He gave me an earful.

COMPLAINING ABOUT A CO-WORKER
抱怨公司同事

Justin, from the marketing department, is complaining to Mary about Joe. Joe is always nasty to Justin and Justin is sick of it. Mary advises Justin not to let Joe bother him.

Mary: How did the meeting with Joe go?

Justin: Lousy. He was **in a snit**.

Mary: Why?

Justin: He **got bent out of shape** over the fact that I didn't bring him the sales *forecasts*. He **gave me an earful** about how people from the marketing department never bring him the right information.

Mary: Don't worry about him. Don't let him **push your buttons**.

Justin: I'll just have to **steer clear of him** now that I know he's such a **hot-head**.

Mary: He's **not a bad guy**, but **he does have issues**. And he's **got a chip on his shoulder** when it comes to marketing people.

Justin: Joe's always **on his high horse** about something.

Mary: You'll just have to **grin and bear it**. We've got a lot of personalities around here.* You'll just have to learn to work with them.

Justin: Well, I don't know how I'm going to be able to work with him. He **gets under my skin**.

* This is a nice way of saying: Many of the people working here have strange and/or unusual personalities, and it may be difficult to work with them.

in a snit 情緒欠佳／不爽
in a bad mood; angry

EXAMPLE: No wonder Donna's **in a snit**. She just found out she didn't get the promotion she was expecting.

(to be or to get) bent out of shape 勃然大怒／發怒
to be or to get very angry about something

EXAMPLE: When Nick's boss told him he couldn't take two weeks off for a vacation, he **got bent out of shape**.

(to) give somebody an earful 數落某人
to say what you really think, in detail (usually criticism and often more than the other person wants to hear)

EXAMPLE: When Doug showed up for work late again, his boss **gave him an earful**.

(to) push one's buttons 惹火某人
to annoy someone; to make someone angry

EXAMPLE: Liz **pushes my buttons** with her bossy behavior.

(to) steer clear of somebody or something 避開⋯⋯
to avoid or stay away from someone or something

EXAMPLE: Ray is on a low-carb diet. He needs to **steer clear of** bread and pasta and other foods high in carbohydrates.

hot-head 脾氣火爆的人
a bad tempered or very moody person; a violent person

EXAMPLE: Don't feel bad that Tim yelled at you. He's a real **hot-head**, and he yells at people all the time.

not a bad guy 人不壞
an okay person (usually used when you don't really like somebody, but you want to say that they're basically not a bad person)

EXAMPLE: Tim does have a bad temper, but he's **not a bad guy**.

(to) have (some) issues　個性有點問題

to have some personality problems (a vague way of saying that somebody is not quite right in some way)

EXAMPLE: Unfortunately, Denise can be difficult to work with. She **has some issues**.

(to) have a chip on one's shoulder　心存芥蒂

to remain angry about a past insult; to bear a grudge

EXAMPLE: Ever since Mike was told he had to leave his office and move into a cubicle, he's **had a chip on his shoulder**.

ORIGIN: This expression comes from the 19th century. Those looking for a fight placed a chip on their shoulder. If an opponent knocked it off, the fight was on. Although that custom has ended, we still say an angry person has a chip on his or her shoulder.

(to be or to get) on one's high horse　自以為高人一等、無所不能

to have an arrogant or superior attitude; to think one has all the answers

EXAMPLE: Hank's **on his high horse** again, telling everybody around him how to behave.

NOTE: You'll also hear the related expression: "Get off your high horse!" meaning to stop acting arrogant or superior.

(to) grin and bear it　忍一忍

to put up with it; to pretend it doesn't bother you

EXAMPLE: I know you don't like traveling with your boss, but it'll just be a short trip. Just **grin and bear it**.

NOTE: "Grin" is another word for smile. "Bear" is to endure or tolerate.

(to) get under one's skin　惹毛某人

to bother; to irritate; to annoy

EXAMPLE: Your boss is certainly annoying, but don't let him **get under your skin**!

115

✎ PRACTICE THE IDIOMS

Fill in the blanks, using the following idioms.

issues with her	get bent out of shape
gets under his skin	hot-head
grin and bear it	in a snit
push my buttons	steer clear

Tracy has a reputation for having a bad temper. Everybody in the office knows she is a ____(1)____. When she's in a bad mood, it's best to just ____(2)____ of her. Seth doesn't like Tracy. He has ____(3)____. He complained to their boss, Yuri, about how much she ____(4)____. "Too bad," said Yuri. "You have to work with her even though you don't like her, so just ____(5)____."

Today, Seth went into Tracy's office and asked her to help him gather some sales data. "Why should I?" asked Tracy. Seth replied, "Why are you ____(6)____ ? This is a simple task. There's no need to ____(7)____ just because I'm asking for your help." Tracy got angry, pounded her fist on her desk, and yelled, "Seth, you really know how to ____(8)____ ! I'm sick and tired of doing *your* job all the time. If you want sales data, get it yourself!"

ANSWERS TO LESSON 19, p. 202

TALKING ABOUT A BROWN NOSER
Part 1
談論辦公室的馬屁精

Nearly every office has one: the brown noser. He or she will do just about anything to win favor with the boss. Here, Tony, Karen, and Nancy complain about their local brown noser, Mitch.

Tony: I was just in a meeting with Mitch and Bill. Mitch said to Bill, "Bill, we're so lucky to have you as our boss. You're such a great leader!"

Karen: He's **up to his old tricks**. He was trying to earn **brownie points** with Bill.

Nancy: Mitch has the reputation of being a **yes man** and a **brown noser**. He's an expert at **kissing up**.

Tony: Then he said to Bill, "Other people here don't appreciate you like I do!" **Talk about** trying to **butter up** the boss!

Nancy: Yeah, and this time **at our expense**! He's just **out for himself**.

Karen: Well, it's a **dog-eat-dog world**. Obviously he thinks this is the way to **get ahead.**

Tony: I guess it's one way to **climb the corporate ladder**. But I could never **look at myself in the mirror** after behaving that way.

Karen: I'm not good at **kissing up** either. **No wonder** I've been in the same lousy position for 10 years!

IDIOMS & EXPRESSIONS - LESSON 20
Part 1

up to one's old tricks
see Lesson 18

---

brownie points 屈意奉承得到的好處跟認同
credit for doing a good deed or for giving someone a compliment (usually a boss or teacher)

EXAMPLE: Sara scored **brownie points** with her boss by volunteering to organize the company's holiday party.

ORIGIN: The junior branch of the Girl Scouts is called the Brownies. Brownies earn credit to then earn a badge by doing good deeds and tasks. When applied to adults, the meaning is sarcastic.

---

yes man 唯唯諾諾的應聲蟲
an employee who always agrees with the boss or does whatever the boss says

EXAMPLE: Don't expect Larry to argue with the boss. He's a **yes man**.

---

brown noser 馬屁精
somebody who's always trying to win favor with those in authority, like bosses or teachers

EXAMPLE: Jim told Amanda she was the best boss he ever had? What a **brown noser**!

(to) kiss up to (someone) 拍馬屁
to try to win favor with someone by flattering them

EXAMPLE: Don is always **kissing up to** the boss. He'll probably get promoted soon.

---

talk about 這就是
that's an example of...

EXAMPLE: Sharon told everybody that Carla was having an affair with her boss. **Talk about** spreading nasty rumors!

118

(to) butter up 阿諛奉承

to say nice things to somebody, hoping that they'll do something nice for you in the future; to compliment too much

EXAMPLE: Sam is trying to get promoted by **buttering up** his boss. His co-workers don't like his behavior.

----

at one's expense 犧牲……的利益

at a cost to

EXAMPLE: If you blame the project failure on us, you'll look better, but **at our expense**.

NOTE: There is also the related expression "at one's own expense," meaning to pay the cost oneself. Example: Fred wanted the job so badly, he was willing to fly to Atlanta for the interview **at his own expense**.

----

out for oneself 只為自己

selfish; just concerned with oneself and one's own success; not caring about what happens to other people

EXAMPLE: : I'm not surprised that Jessica took all the credit for the success of the ad campaign. She's just **out for herself**.

----

dog-eat-dog world 人吃人的世界

a cruel and aggressive world in which people just look out for themselves

EXAMPLE: Your company fired you shortly after you had a heart attack? Well, it's certainly a **dog-eat-dog world**!

ORIGIN: This expression dates back to the 1500's. Wild dogs were observed fighting aggressively over a piece of food. The connection was made that people, like dogs, often compete aggressively to get what they want.

(to) get ahead 升遷

to get promoted; to advance in one's career

EXAMPLE: If you want to **get ahead** in investment banking, be prepared to work long hours!

(to) climb the corporate ladder 升遷／晉升

advance in one's career; the process of getting promoted and making it to senior management

EXAMPLE: You want to **climb the corporate ladder**? It helps to be productive and to look good in front of your boss.

....

(to) look at oneself in the mirror 面對自己

to face oneself

EXAMPLE: After firing so many employees, I don't know how Beth can even **look at herself in the mirror**.

....

no wonder
see Lesson 7

Talking About a Brown Noser, Part 2: When You're Overheard
（談話內容被當事人聽到了）

Mitch: Hey guys. Don't you know it's rude to **talk behind someone's back**? I just overheard your entire conversation!

Tony: Sorry, Mitch. We didn't mean to offend you.

Mitch: Well, **the walls have ears**. **Think twice** before you insult me again!

Nancy: **Chill out!** We were talking about a different Mitch, not you.

Tony: That's right. We were talking about Mitch Schneider, over in the accounting department.

Mitch: **Likely story. I wasn't born yesterday!**

(to) talk behind someone's back 背後議論某人

to gossip about somebody; to say negative things about somebody who's not around

EXAMPLE: Please don't **talk behind my back**. If you have something to say to me, say it to my face.

the walls have ears 隔牆有耳

you never know when somebody might be listening to your "private" conversation

EXAMPLE: Don't complain about the boss while we're in the office. Remember, **the walls have ears**!

(to) think twice 三思

to think more carefully before doing something in the future; to not repeat a mistake one has made

EXAMPLE: Jane didn't even thank you for your Christmas gift? You should **think twice** before giving her a gift next year!

Chill out! 別緊張

Relax! Don't worry!

EXAMPLE: **Chill out!** Your presentation to the CEO will go fine.

likely story 鬼才相信／真的才怪

that's not true; I find that hard to believe

EXAMPLE: When Jim and Jenny were caught kissing each other in the conference room, they said it would never happen again. That's a **likely story**!

I wasn't born yesterday! 我又不是三歲小孩

I'm not stupid; I'm not naive

EXAMPLE: I just got an e-mail from a company promising to send me $10 million next year if I send them $10,000 now. Too bad for them **I wasn't born yesterday!**

✒ PRACTICE THE IDIOMS

Choose the most appropriate response to the following:

1) We'd better be careful what we say in the office.
    a) That's right. The walls have ears.
    b) Likely story!
    c) Right, I wasn't born yesterday.

2) Josh, we're going to have to ask you to take a 40 percent pay cut. But next year, I promise we'll triple your salary.
    a) Lower your voice. The walls have ears!
    b) Don't get too excited. Chill out!
    c) That's hard to believe. I wasn't born yesterday!

3) Megan is constantly flattering her boss and offering to do favors for him.
    a) Why doesn't she butter him up instead?
    b) Think twice before accepting favors from her.
    c) That's one way to climb the corporate ladder.

4) I'm giving a presentation to our CEO in a half an hour. I'm so nervous!
    a) Likely story.
    b) Chill out!
    c) You're such a yes man.

5) I spent three hours helping Bob with his financial projections, and he didn't even say thank you.
    a) You need to look at yourself in the mirror.
    b) I'm sure you'll think twice before helping him again.
    c) He's trying to climb the corporate ladder.

6) Maria works at least 60 hours a week at the law firm and always volunteers for extra work. She's an excellent employee.
    a) She'll definitely get ahead.
    b) Let's not talk about her behind her back.
    c) It's a dog-eat-dog world.

7) Paul was arrested for stealing millions of dollars from his company.
   a) I'm not surprised. He's a real yes man.
   b) That's one way to climb the corporate ladder.
   c) I don't know how he can look at himself in the mirror.

8) You're the best boss I've ever had and definitely the smartest!
   a) Are you just out for yourself?
   b) Are you trying to butter me up?
   c) Isn't it a dog-eat-dog world?

ANSWERS TO LESSON 20, p. 202

Fill in the blank with the missing word:

1) After he was fired, Roger was going to send a nasty e-mail to his boss. But then he changed his mind and decided not to _____ his bridges.

   a) break   b) burn   c) destroy

2) Courtney's department is very efficient. She really runs a tight _____.

   a) ship   b) boat   c) raft

3) After spending several weeks out of the office, Phil felt _____ the loop.

   a) part of   b) in   c) out of

4) Jeremy brought his boss Betsy flowers on Boss's Day. He's always trying to _____ her up.

   a) please   b) oil   c) butter

5) If you bought a house closer to your office, you could _____ a bundle on gas.

   a) spare   b) save   c) make

6) Ever since Sam was passed up for a promotion last fall, he's had a chip on his _____.

   a) arm   b) shoulder   c) elbow

7) We need to think of some creative ways to increase our sales. Let's get together and bat _____ some ideas.

   a) around   b) about   c) off

8) You didn't reply to my urgent e-mail because your computer wasn't work-ing? Spare me the _____ story!

   a) tragic   b) sad   c) sob

9) According to the rumor _____, Wayne has been having an affair with his administrative assistant for the past twenty years.

   a) mill   b) bin   c) machine

10) Zachary showed up late for work again, and then claimed he had a dentist appointment. He's up to his _____ tricks.

   a) new   b) old   c) favorite

11) I know you're not enjoying your international assignment, but you'll be leaving in a few months. For now, you'll just have to _____ and bear it.

   a) grin   b) smile   c) laugh

12) Roy is in charge of sales at our company, and our sales are down by 75 percent versus last year. His days are _____.

   a) limited   b) lettered   c) numbered

13) If you want to get _____ at this company, you're going to have to kiss up to your boss and put in long hours like everybody else.

   a) up   b) forward   c) ahead

14) You can try to talk me into going to the conference until you're _____ in the face. I've already decided I'm not going.

   a) green   b) blue   c) red

15) When Shane was told he would have to move into a much smaller office, he got really _____ out of shape.

   a) twisted   b) bent   c) stretched

ANSWERS TO REVIEW, p. 203

I don't know whether I'm coming or going.

EXPLAINING THAT YOU'RE FEELING OVERWORKED
說明自己工作負擔過重

Mary is feeling overwhelmed between commitments at home and at work. Dan advises her to be patient and stay focused. Things will improve once their busy period at the office is over.

Dan: Mary, why weren't you at the staff meeting this morning? We all missed you.

Mary: Oh, it completely **slipped my mind**.

Dan: How could you forget? These meetings are not *optional*.

Mary: I'm feeling so **stressed out** these days. Sometimes **I don't know whether I'm coming or going**!

Dan: Well, it *is* **crunch time** right now. Things will **settle down** after tax season is over.

Mary: I hope so. I am **wiped out** after putting in 60-hour weeks at the office and taking care of my five kids and sick mother.

Dan: Wow, you really do **have a lot on your plate**.

Mary: Yeah, I can hardly **keep my head above water**. Maybe I should **scale back my hours**.

Dan: Just **hang in there** a little longer. After April 15th, it'll quiet down around here. For now, **keep your nose to the grindstone** and focus on getting your most important work done.

Mary: You're right. I need to remember the **80/20 rule**. I get 80 percent of my results from just 20 percent of my activities. Now if I could only figure out what that 20 percent is!

IDIOMS & EXPRESSIONS - LESSON 21

slip one's mind　一時忘記
be forgotten

EXAMPLE: Sorry I didn't send out that memo last Friday. To be honest with you, it **slipped my mind**.

NOTE: Notice that the subject is "it" in the expression "it slipped my mind," making this the passive voice. It's like this unknown "it" is responsible for the fact that you forgot to do something. In contrast, "I forgot" is the active voice. You are taking more responsibility (and possibly more blame) when you say, "I forgot."

stressed out　壓力很大
under severe strain; very anxious; very nervous

EXAMPLE: After hearing a rumor that there were going to be layoffs at her company, Barbara was really **stressed out**.

I don't know whether I'm coming or going　頭腦不清楚
I'm so busy, I can barely think clearly; I'm not focused; I'm distracted

EXAMPLE: I accidentally sent an e-mail complaining about my boss to the boss himself! **I don't whether I'm coming or going** today.

crunch time　緊要關頭／關鍵時刻
a short period when there's high pressure to achieve a result

EXAMPLE: It's **crunch time** for stem cell researchers in Korea. New government regulations may soon make their work illegal.

(to) settle down 平息／回穩
to calm down; to become quiet

EXAMPLE: The mall is very busy in November and December, but after the holidays, things **settle down**.

wiped out 筋疲力竭
very tired; exhausted

EXAMPLE: Ken traveled to Russia, India, and China all in one week. No wonder he's **wiped out**!

(to) have a lot on one's plate 有許多事要處理
to have a lot to do; to have too much to do; to have too much to cope with

EXAMPLE: Carlos turned down the project, explaining that he already **had a lot on his plate**.

NOTE: There is also the variation: to have too much on one's plate.

(to) keep one's head above water 喘息／撐過去
to survive; to get by; to survive financial difficulties

EXAMPLE: Thanks to this new contract, we'll be able to **keep our head above water** for another six months.

(to) scale back one's hours 減少工時
to reduce the number of hours one works

EXAMPLE: When Christine had a baby, she decided to **scale back her hours** and just work part-time.

SYNONYM: to cut back one's hours

hang in there 加油／別氣餒
be patient; don't get discouraged

EXAMPLE: Your company lost a million dollars last quarter? **Hang in there**. You'll do better next quarter.

(to) keep one's nose to the grindstone 專心工作
to focus on one's work; to focus on working hard

EXAMPLE: Unfortunately, I can't come to happy hour tonight. I need to **keep my nose to the grindstone** and finish a proposal I'm working on.

ORIGIN: A grindstone is a stone disk used for sharpening tools or grinding grain. To work the grindstone, you need to bend over it with your nose close to the stone.

(the) 80/20 rule 80/20法則
the principle that 80 percent of results are achieved through just 20 percent of activities

EXAMPLE: By applying the **80/20 rule**, Marcy was able to reduce the number of tasks she does during the work day.

✎ PRACTICE THE IDIOMS

Choose the best substitute for the phrase or sentence in bold:

1) Kate said she didn't have time to help you? I'm not surprised, since **she has a lot on her plate right now**.
   a) she's very busy these days
   b) she's taken too much food
   c) she doesn't really like to help people

2) Instead of retiring, Joyce decided to keep working and just **scale back her hours**.
   a) increase the number of hours she works
   b) retire in a few years
   c) reduce the number of hours she works

3) You've been at the office every night until midnight for the past three months? **Hang in there.** In just a few more weeks, the busy period will probably be over.
   a) Quit your job.
   b) Be patient.
   c) Keep complaining.

4) Tanya works all day and goes to school every evening. No wonder she's **wiped out**.
   a) exhausted
   b) sick
   c) full of energy

5) At the tax consulting firm, March and April are **crunch time**.
   a) a relaxing time
   b) a slow period
   c) a very busy period

6) You asked me to buy you a bamboo vase on my business trip to Hanoi? I'm sorry, but **it slipped my mind**!
   a) you never asked me for that
   b) I forgot
   c) I didn't get a chance

7) Eva is working full-time while studying for her MBA and taking care of her two small kids. **I don't know how she can keep her head above water.**
   a) No wonder she has no time to go swimming.
   b) I don't know how she manages.
   c) I don't know what she does with all her free time.

8) If you want to pass the CPA exam, you'd better **keep your nose to the grindstone** and stop going out every night to party.
   a) focus on studying
   b) focus on having fun
   c) keep your nose out of other people's business

ANSWERS TO LESSON 21, p. 203

My stomach is killing me.

CALLING IN SICK
請病假

Maria calls her boss, Scott, to tell him she's not feeling well and that she's going to have to take a sick day. Fortunately, Scott is an understanding boss.

Maria: Hi, Scott, it's Maria.

Scott: Hey Maria. **What's up?**

Maria: I'm not feeling well today.

Scott: Oh yeah? What's wrong?

Maria: **My stomach is killing me**. Maybe it's the sushi I ate last night. I'm **as sick as a dog**.

Scott: Sara **called in sick** today also. And Kurt just told me he was feeling **under the weather** today. I'm **not feeling so hot** myself. Maybe **there's something going around**.

Maria: Well, I hope you don't catch it too.

Scott: I **can't afford to** get sick. I'm **up to my ears** in work.

Maria: I should be back in the office tomorrow.

Scott: Don't worry about that. You should stay home until you feel better.

Maria: I'll try to work from home this afternoon if I feel better.

Scott: **Take it easy** today. We want you back **in tip-top shape**.

What's up?

1) What's happening? What's new?　近來如何

EXAMPLE: **What's up?** I haven't seen you in a long time.

2) A polite way of asking "What do you want?" when somebody calls or comes into your office.　有什麼事

EXAMPLE: **"What's up?"** — "I came by to see if you're free for lunch today."

......

my stomach *(my head, my arm, etc…)* is killing me　我胃（頭、手臂…等）疼得不得了

my stomach (my head, my arm, etc…) hurts very badly

EXAMPLE: Patricia left the office early today. **Her stomach was killing her.**

......

as sick as a dog　病懨懨

EXAMPLE: Brent got the flu and was **as sick as a dog** for a week.

......

(to) call in sick　請病假

to phone into the office and say you're sick

EXAMPLE: Try not to **call in sick** too often. Employers don't like it.

......

under the weather　感覺不適

not feeling well

EXAMPLE: "You look pale. Is everything okay?" — "Not really. I'm feeling **under the weather.**"

......

(to) not feel so hot　感覺不舒服

to feel sick; to not feel well

EXAMPLE: Jacob canceled our meeting for this afternoon. He said he **wasn't feeling so hot.**

there's something going around 辦公室裡有病菌

there's an illness traveling around the office; many people are getting sick from some illness

EXAMPLE: Be sure to wash your hands often. **There's something going around the office**, and you don't want to catch it.

can't afford to 沒時間……／可不想……

don't have time for; don't want to

EXAMPLE: Sorry, I **can't afford to** sit here and argue with you. I've got a lot of work to do.

up to one's ears in work 工作堆積如山

to have a lot of work; to have too much work

EXAMPLE: Bill is **up to his ears in work**. He won't be able to meet with you until next week.

(to) take it easy 放鬆休息

to relax; to rest; to not do too much

EXAMPLE: You worry too much about everything. You need to just **take it easy**.

in tip-top shape 健健康康／好好的

in great condition; completely healthy

EXAMPLE: Be sure you're **in tip-top shape** next week for our trip to Beijing.

✎ Practice the Idioms

Fill in the blanks, using the following idioms:

killing me	take it easy
in tip-top shape	under the weather
up to my ears in work	call in sick
I'm not feeling so hot	there's something going around

Diana woke up this morning feeling ____(1)____. "What's wrong?" her husband Boris asked. "My head is ____(2)____," she replied. Boris handed her the phone and suggested that she ____(3)____. "But I can't stay home today. I've got too much to do at the office," she said. "I'm ____(4)____." Boris told her that the work could wait.

Diana took the phone and called her boss. "____(5)____," said Diana. Her boss replied, "It looks like ____(6)____ the office. Several other people have also called in sick today. Just ____(7)____ today and hopefully tomorrow you'll be ____(8)____." Diana was grateful that she had such an understanding boss. She rolled over and went back to sleep.

ANSWERS TO LESSON 22, p. 203

REQUESTING A BANK LOAN
申請銀行貸款

Ivan meets with Gina, a loan officer at L&S Bank, about getting a loan to start a new coffee shop. When Gina reviews his financial forecasts and suggests some changes, Ivan is angry at first but then decides to go along with it.

Ivan: I'm here to see about getting a $100,000 loan to start a Coffee Shack *franchise*.

Gina: I see from your application that you've already got two franchise businesses **under your belt** — both Subway sandwich shops. That's certainly **nothing to sneeze at**.

Ivan: Thank you. Now that I **know the franchise business inside and out**, I'd like to expand.

Gina: Well, Subway is a sandwich shop. Now you're talking about a coffee house. That's an entirely **different animal**.

Ivan: Sure, there may be a thing or two to learn, but it should be more or less a **no-brainer**.

Gina: I see from your business plan that you're basing all of your profit estimates on the profits you made from one of your Subway shops. I don't think that's right. You're **comparing apples to oranges**.

Ivan: Apples? Oranges? I didn't know we were talking about fruit now. Maybe I should open up a *fruit smoothie* shop instead!

Gina: Ha ha. Well, at least you haven't lost your sense of humor!

Ivan: Well, seriously, what do you want me to do?

Gina: Go **back to the drawing board**. Make some new calculations based on selling coffee, not sandwiches. Then the loan will be **in the bag**.

Ivan: If you're going to make me **jump through hoops** to get this loan, I'll just have to take my business to a different bank.

Gina: You're **missing the point** here. I'm not trying to make your life difficult. I'm just suggesting you **beef up** your business plan so my boss will approve your loan.

Ivan: Well, in that case, maybe I will go **back to the drawing board**.

IDIOMS & EXPRESSIONS - LESSON 23

(to get or to have) under one's belt　有經驗
to get or to have experience

EXAMPLE: Before you start your own coffee shop, you should work at Starbucks to **get some experience under your belt**.

. . . .

nothing to sneeze at　不簡單
not insignificant; impressive

EXAMPLE: This year, our company opened 15 new sales offices overseas. That's **nothing to sneeze at**!

. . . .

(to) know something inside and out　熟悉／在行
to know something very well

EXAMPLE: If you're having a problem with your presentation, ask Pam for help. She **knows PowerPoint inside and out**.

different animal　不同的事物
something entirely different

EXAMPLE: The Gap had many years of experience selling clothing through retail stores. When they started the Gap.com, they found out that selling online was a **different animal**.

no-brainer　輕而易舉之決定
an easy decision; an obvious choice

EXAMPLE: Most of our clients are based in Korea, so it's a **no-brainer** to open an office there.

(to) compare apples to oranges　比較的事物不同
to compare two unlike things; to make an invalid comparison

EXAMPLE: Comparing a night at EconoLodge with a night at the Four Seasons is like **comparing apples to oranges**. One is a budget motel, and the other is a luxury hotel.

NOTE: You will also see the related expression "compare apples to apples" which means to compare two things of the same type. This means that you are making a valid comparison, as opposed to when you're comparing apples to oranges.

(to) go back to the drawing board　重新來過
to start a task over because the last try failed; to start again from the beginning

EXAMPLE: We didn't like the print advertisement our ad agency designed, so we asked them to **go back to the drawing board**.

in the bag　探囊取物／囊中之物
a sure thing

EXAMPLE: Boeing executives thought that the new military contract was **in the bag** and were surprised when it was awarded to Airbus instead.

SYNONYM: a done deal. Example: Boeing executives thought the new military contract was **a done deal**.

(to) jump through hoops 過五關斬六將／經歷一堆複雜的程序
to go through a lot of difficult work for something; to face many bureaucratic obstacles

EXAMPLE: We had to **jump through hoops** to get our visas to Russia, but we finally got them.

(to) miss the point 搞錯了／沒弄清楚
to not understand

EXAMPLE: You're **missing the point**. Your son wants an expensive new cell phone so he can impress his friends, not because he actually needs all of those bells and whistles.

beef up – see Lesson 5

✎ PRACTICE THE IDIOMS

Choose the best substitute for the phrase or sentence in bold:

1) Procter & Gamble had to **jump through hoops** to get its new drug approved by the Food and Drug Administration.
   a) ask the right people
   b) take many steps
   c) show proven results

2) Nora had a very good job interview with the bank. She thinks **the job is in the bag.**
   a) she'll get an offer
   b) she'll get a rejection letter
   c) she'll get a bag with the bank's logo on it

3) Madeleine Albright made many connections while she was U.S. Secretary of State. It was **a no-brainer** for her to open a political consulting firm after she left office.
   a) a poor decision
   b) a logical decision
   c) a tough decision

4) When the popular coffee house announced it would start staying open until midnight and start serving beer, many loyal customers feared it would **become a different animal**.
   a) become a hangout for dogs and cats
   b) change in character
   c) become an even better coffee house

5) I know you were hoping for a higher bonus, but $5,000 is **nothing to sneeze at!**
   a) less than you deserve
   b) disappointing
   c) a good amount of money

6) Of course, I prefer Dom Perignon champagne over a $4 bottle of sparking wine, but **comparing the two is like comparing apples to oranges**.
   a) you can't really compare the two
   b) one is fruitier than the other
   c) it makes sense to compare the two

7) If you need advice on where to set up your new manufacturing facility in China, talk to Stan. **He knows China inside and out.**
   a) He's been to China a few times.
   b) He speaks Chinese.
   c) He knows China very well.

8) Chris spent a year working as an intern at Chelsea Brewing Company in order to **get some experience under his belt**. Then he opened his own microbrewery.
   a) have a good time
   b) make some money
   c) gain experience

ANSWERS TO LESSON 23, p. 203

You really need a full page ad to make a splash.

NEGOTIATING A PURCHASE
買賣交涉

Jack, owner of Jack's Party Store, is negotiating to buy an advertisement in the Newport Times. Dave is an ad salesman with the newspaper.

Jack: My store is having a big sale next week. I'd like to buy a small advertisement in the Sunday edition of the *Newport Times*. How much would a quarter page cost?

Dave: A quarter page ad costs $250. What you really need is a full page ad if you want to **make a splash**. That would be $900. I better reserve that for you before we run out of space.

Jack: Don't try to give me **the hard sell**. Nine hundred bucks would **break my budget**!

Dave: Okay, so we're looking at a quarter page. For another $200 I can make it a full color ad. Color would give you **more bang for the buck**.

Jack: Of course color is better than black and white. That's a **no-brainer**! Can you **throw that in at no extra charge**?

Dave: Sorry, **no can do**.

Jack: Your competitor, the *Newport Bulletin*, is offering me a quarter page color ad for $300. That's very attractive since I'm **on a tight budget**.

Dave: The *Newport Bulletin?* This is **off the record**, but you really don't want to advertise in that *rag!* Nobody reads it.

Jack: Here's my final offer: I'll take a quarter page color ad in your paper for $350 and not a penny more.

Dave: How about we find a **happy medium**. I'll give it to you for $400.

Jack: Please don't try to **nickel-and-dime** me. I'm **standing firm** at $350.

Dave: Okay, I don't want to spend all afternoon arguing. **It's a deal**.

IDIOMS & EXPRESSIONS - LESSON 24

(to) make a splash 引起注意
to make a big impact; to get a lot of attention

EXAMPLE: Careerbuilder.com **made a splash** with its funny TV commercials starring chimpanzees.

(the) hard sell 強迫推銷
an aggressive way of selling

EXAMPLE: Car salesmen are famous for using **the hard sell** on their customers.

NOTE: The opposite of "the hard sell" is "the soft sell," which is a sales technique using little or no pressure.

(to) break one's budget 超出預算
to cost much more than one wants to pay; to cost more than one can afford

EXAMPLE: The advertising expenses you proposed are too high. We don't want to **break our budget**.

more bang for the buck 投資更有報酬／錢花得更有價值
more value for one's money; a higher return on investment

EXAMPLE: We should add some more features to our products. Customers are starting to demand **more bang for the buck**.

NOTE: A "buck" is slang for a "dollar."

---

no-brainer
see Lesson 23

(to) throw in something 包含／涵蓋
to include something (usually for free, as part of the sale)

EXAMPLE: Order our new exercise equipment today, and we'll **throw in** a free how-to video.

---

at no extra charge 不另加收費用／免費
for free; for no additional money

EXAMPLE: If you buy a ticket to the museum, you can visit the special Van Gogh exhibit **at no extra charge**.

---

no can do 愛莫能助／做不到
I can't do that; I'm unable to satisfy your request

EXAMPLE: "We'd like you to work on Thanksgiving Day this year." — "Sorry, **no can do**. I've already got plans."

(to be) on a tight budget 預算有限
to not have much money to spend; to have a limited amount to spend

EXAMPLE: Can you give us a better price on the printing job? We're **on a tight budget**.

---

off the record 檯面下的事／不可外洩
just between us; unofficial; not to be repeated to others

EXAMPLE: This is **off the record**, but I wouldn't trust Todd to do the financial analysis. He's careless and often makes mistakes.

happy medium　折衷
a compromise

EXAMPLE: Lee wants to spend $100,000 re-designing our entire website, while Nicole suggests just adding a few new links. We need to find a **happy medium**.

....

(to) nickel-and-dime　斤斤計較小數字／講價
to negotiate over very small sums; to try to get a better financial deal, in a negative way

EXAMPLE: We don't want to **nickel-and-dime** you, but we'd really appreciate it if you would lower your estimate by another $250.

ORIGIN: After the penny, nickels and dimes are the smallest units of U.S. currency. Pennies, nickels, and dimes are common words in American English idioms related to money, finances, and value. Other examples of these expressions include:
• pretty penny – see Lesson 9
• dime a dozen – very common and of no special value
• pinch pennies – to be careful with money
• a penny saved is a penny earned – you will save money by being careful about how much you spend; it's wise to save your money

....

(to) stand firm　立場堅定／不退讓
to remain at; to not offer more than; to resist; to refuse to yield to

EXAMPLE: Pemco Industries put a lot of pressure on Peggy to resign, but she **stood firm** and refused to leave her job voluntarily.

....

it's a deal　成交
I agree (to a proposal or offer)

EXAMPLE: "If you let me leave at noon on Friday, I'll stay here late on Thursday." — "Okay, **it's a deal**."

✒ PRACTICE THE IDIOMS

Fill in the blanks, using the following idioms:

> the hard sell   it's a deal
> no can do   at no extra charge
> more bang for the buck   break my budget
> nickel-and-dime   on a tight budget

Tina: Hi, I'm in the market for a new car, and I like the Mini Cooper. Would you recommend the base model or the Cooper S model?

Eric: The Cooper S. It gives you _____(1)_____. It's got a lot more power. I would also suggest you upgrade to leather seats.

Tina: How much extra are those?

Eric: $1300.

Tina: Forget it! That's too much. It would _____(2)_____.

Eric: Okay, I'm just making a suggestion. I'm not trying to give you _____(3)_____ . However, you probably will want to get the heated front seats.

Tina: Can you throw those in _____(4)_____?

Eric: Sorry, _____(5)_____.

Tina: Well, how much would the car cost without all the bells and whistles?

Eric: $20,500.

Tina: I don't want to _____(6)_____ you, but I am a single mother with four kids and I'm _____(7)_____. Can you offer it to me for $18,500?

Eric: I'm afraid not. But I could go to $19,500.

Tina: Okay, _____(8)_____.

ANSWERS TO LESSON 24, p. 203

You've got a knack for sales.

CONDUCTING A PERFORMANCE REVIEW
檢視員工績效

It's annual performance review time. John meets with his boss to go over his performance for the past year, hear about his strengths and weaknesses, and find out about his salary increase.

Sara: During the first half of the year, your performance was **not so hot**. But then you **did a 180** and you started doing great.

John: Really? I was that bad at the beginning of the year?

Sara: I think it was because you were new here, and it took you a while **to get up to speed**. The most important thing is that you're now a valuable member of the team.

John: That's nice to hear.

Sara: You've **got a knack for** sales. These past few months, I've also seen your communication skills improve. You're great at **keeping people in the loop** and making sure we all know what's going on with your accounts.

John: Thanks. I do **pride myself on** my communication skills.

Sara: Of course, you still have some **opportunity areas** that I'd like you to work on, starting with your *analytical* skills. Sometimes I can't **make heads or tails of** your sales forecasts.

John: How would you suggest I work on that?

Sara: I'm going to send you to a training class. Then we'll **take it from there**.

John: Great. I love attending classes!

Sara: We'll be raising your salary by 5 percent to $60,000. And, if you really go **beyond the call of duty**, you'll also receive a bonus at the end of the year.

IDIOMS & EXPRESSIONS - LESSON 25

not so hot 不佳
not very good

EXAMPLE: This new advertising campaign is **not so hot**. I think we can do better next time.

(to) do a 180 一百八十度大轉變
to turn around; to change position completely; to improve a lot

EXAMPLE: The electronics company used to insist on manufacturing its products in the USA, but then they **did a 180**. Now all of their products are made in China.

NOTE: This phrase refers to 180 degrees (half of the 360 degrees of a circle). If you turn 180 degrees, you've moved to the opposite direction.

(to) get up to speed 工作上軌道
to learn how to do a new job or a new task

EXAMPLE: Leo had to start making sales calls his first week on the job, so he didn't have much time to **get up to speed**.

(to) have a knack for something 對⋯⋯很在行／拿手
to be skilled at something; to be naturally good at something (either in a positive or a negative way)

EXAMPLE: I can't believe Joe told you that your tie looks old-fashioned. He **has a knack for** making people feel bad.

(to) keep someone in the loop 隨時讓某人知道最新狀況
to let someone know what's going on; to provide regular updates

EXAMPLE: The finance manager doesn't need to be invited to every meeting, but be sure to **keep her in the loop**.

(to) pride oneself on something 以⋯⋯自豪
to be proud of; to recognize one's own skill in a certain area

EXAMPLE: Naomi **prides herself on** her excellent people skills.

opportunity areas　弱項／尚待改進之處
weaknesses; skills that need to be improved

EXAMPLE: The human resource manager spent 45 minutes with Kristen, reviewing her **opportunity areas**.

(to) not be able to make heads or tails of　看不懂／不瞭解
to be unable to interpret

EXAMPLE: Magna Corporation's new employee health plan is very confusing. The employees **can't make heads or tails of it**.

(to) take it from there　到時再視情況而定
to wait and see what else needs to be done; to take just one step and then decide what to do next

EXAMPLE: Let's start by calculating how much it would cost to open an office in Budapest, and then we'll **take it from there**.

---

beyond the call of duty　表現超乎預期／出色
more than is expected or required

EXAMPLE: Susan worked all day Sunday baking chocolate chip cookies for the office. That was **beyond the call of duty**.

NOTE: You will also hear the variation: above and beyond the call of duty.

✎ PRACTICE THE IDIOMS

Choose the best substitute for the phrase or sentence in bold:

1) Susan said she'd be happy to bring chocolate chip cookies to the office. **She prides herself on being a good baker.**
   a) She mistakenly thinks she can bake.
   b) She's proud of her skills as a baker.
   c) She bakes chocolate chip cookies every day.

2) Al's attitude was bad last year, but this year he's **done a 180**.
   a) developed an even worse attitude
   b) dramatically improved his attitude
   c) left the job

3) The new government regulations are very complicated. **We can't make heads or tails of them.**
   a) We think they're excellent.
   b) We think they're very bad.
   c) We can't understand them at all.

4) Although you've improved your written communication skills over the past year, this is still an **opportunity area for you**.
   a) an area where you need to improve further
   b) an area where you've already made enough progress
   c) an area where you'll find exciting opportunities

5) If you need help with your new logo, ask Molly. **She's got a knack for graphic design**.
   a) She used to be a graphic designer.
   b) She knows several good graphic designers.
   c) She's very good at graphic design.

6) You spent 14 hours proofreading my report? **That was beyond the call of duty**.
   a) That was more than I expected.
   b) You shouldn't have bothered.
   c) You were just doing your job.

7) Please **keep me in the loop regarding** your vacation plans. I need to know when you're not going to be in the office.
   a) keep me updated about
   b) don't bother telling me about
   c) let everybody in the office know about

8) Juan's new job at the lab is very complicated. It may take him a few months to **get up to speed**.
   a) feel like he's got too much work to do
   b) feel comfortable doing the job
   c) feel like the job is too difficult for him

ANSWERS TO LESSON 25, p. 203

REVIEW FOR LESSONS 21-25

Fill in the blank with the missing word:

1) Companies shouldn't make investors _____ through hoops to get financial information.

   a) hop   b) skip   c) jump

2) After hosting 25 visitors from Japan for four weeks, Marie was wiped _____.

   a) in   b) out   c) up

3) Jerry suggested that I buy the Dell Pocket DJ instead of the Apple iPod Mini. He said I'd get more bang for the _____.

   a) dollar   b) buck   c) cash

4) The loan officer at the bank said our business plan was very confusing. He couldn't make heads or _____ of it.

   a) tails   b) necks   c) sense

5) I'm sorry I won't be able to come to your presentation. I'm up to my _____ in work.

   a) eyes   b) ears   c) head

6) Sorry I forgot to book your airplane tickets. It _____ my mind.

   a) slipped   b) escaped   c) skipped

7) Oil prices have come down recently, but $50 a barrel is still nothing to _____ at.

   a) laugh   b) sniff   c) sneeze

8) That e-mail you sent me with the details about your project was very helpful. Thanks for keeping me _____ the loop.

   a) within   b) in   c) with

9) Between working full-time at the bank and volunteering as a fireman on weekends, Neil has a lot on his _____.

   a) table   b) plate   c) desk

10) Wal-Mart set up a huge display of under $20 Christmas gifts. It's great for people on a _____ budget.

   a) big   b) loose   c) tight

11) No wonder Ken is so rich. He has a knack _____ picking winning stocks!

   a) for   b) with   c) in

12) When Wendy and Jim bought the leather couch for $1600, the furniture store agreed to throw _____ a $200 chair at no extra charge.

   a) up   b) out   c) in

13) Andy won't be in today. He's feeling _____ the weather.

   a) over   b) under   c) beyond

14) Things have been very busy at the office lately. I hope they'll settle _____ soon.

   a) down   b) over   c) up

15) We want to move our company headquarters to a city. Chicago is too large, but Salt Lake City is too small. Atlanta might be a _____ medium.

   a) perfect   b) happy   c) mixed

ANSWERS TO REVIEW, p. 204

154

PROMOTING AN EMPLOYEE
升職

Steve is meeting with his boss, Kurt, to review his performance. Kurt promotes Steve to the position of marketing director.

Kurt: Steve, your performance over the past year has been excellent. You've only been here a year, but you **hit the ground running**.

Steve: Thank you. It's nice to be appreciated!

Kurt: You're **an "A" player** here — a real star. You've really **earned your keep**. You're great at motivating your employees, and you're always willing to **go the extra mile**.

Steve: Thanks, Kurt. I really enjoy my work here.

Kurt: I'm going to **take you into my confidence**. Steve, this past year has been really challenging. Everybody hasn't **made the grade**.

Steve: Right. I heard that Dan is going to be **given his walking papers.**

Kurt: Yes, he'll be **leaving us**. I'll be **breaking the news** to him this afternoon. But the good news is that I'm promoting you to marketing director.

Steve: Wow, that is good news. Thank you!

Kurt: No need to thank me. You're a real **go-getter** and you earned it. The new position comes with a 10 percent raise and several *perks*, including an extra week of vacation.

Steve: Will I get a company car too?

Kurt: Don't **push your luck.** But if you **play your cards right**, maybe in a few years. Ten years **down the road**, I can even see you in a *corner office.*

Steve: Thanks, Kurt.

Kurt: No, Steve, thank you. **Keep up the good work!**

IDIOMS & EXPRESSIONS - LESSON 26

(to) hit the ground running　馬上勝任工作
to have a successful start to a new job; to start at full speed

EXAMPLE: We need to hire somebody who can **hit the ground running**. We don't have time to train anybody.

(an) "A" player　優秀員工
a top performer; a superior employee

EXAMPLE: We need to do everything we can to ensure that our **"A" players** don't leave our company and take jobs with the competition.

(to) earn one's keep　值得雇用／沒白領薪水
to deserve what one is paid; to deserve to be in the position one is in; to contribute one's share

EXAMPLE: Carl stands around flirting with the receptionist all day instead of working. He's not **earning his keep**.

(to) go the extra mile　做得比本份還多
to do more than what is expected or required

EXAMPLE: The graphic designer showed us 25 possible designs for the cover of our new newsletter. He really **went the extra mile**.

(to) take someone into one's confidence 告訴某人內幕消息
to tell somebody something confidentially; to tell somebody sensitive information

EXAMPLE: Linda **took Dan into her confidence** and told him that several people in the department were going to get laid off.

(to) make the grade 表現優秀／達成目標
to succeed; to fulfill the requirements

EXAMPLE: After it was clear that Nathan **made the grade** as an account executive at the ad agency, he was promoted to account director.

(to) give someone their walking papers 遣散某人／解僱某人
to dismiss someone from work; to tell someone to leave their work

EXAMPLE: If Herb Sendek does not win tonight, it is time for him to either resign or **be given his walking papers**.

leaving us 離職
leaving the company (note: often a polite way of saying somebody's been fired)

EXAMPLE: We're sad to say that after ten years here, Leslie will be **leaving us** to pursue more time with her family.

(to) break the news 通知消息／告知
to make something known (often something unpleasant)

EXAMPLE: Sorry to **break the news**, but your competitors have come out with a product that works much better than yours and costs half the price.

go-getter 積極進取的人
a hard-working, ambitious person; someone very good at delivering results at work

EXAMPLE: Stephanie is a real **go-getter**, so nobody was surprised when she was promoted to vice president of the bank.

(to) push one's luck 得寸進尺

don't try to get too much; be satisfied with what you've already gotten and don't try to get more

EXAMPLE: If your boss has already agreed to send you to two training courses this year, don't **push your luck** and ask for a third.

NOTE: You will also hear the variation: to press one's luck.

(to) play one's cards right 把握善用機會

to make the most of one's opportunities or situation

EXAMPLE: Louis **played his cards right** at the law firm, and he was made partner after only five years there.

down the road 未來

in the future

EXAMPLE: Jay doesn't want to work for a big company forever. Five years **down the road**, he'd like to start his own business.

Keep up the good work! 繼續保持

continue as you are; you're doing well, continue to do well

EXAMPLE: Team, we just had our best year in company history. **Keep up the good work!**

✎ PRACTICE THE IDIOMS

Choose the best substitute for the phrase or sentence in bold:

1) Sonia is **a real go-getter**. No wonder she was our top salesperson last month!
   a) very good at making friends
   b) a reliable, kind person
   c) very effective at her job

2) My company just agreed to give me a company car, so I'm not going to **push my luck** by asking for a large raise now.
   a) see if I can get more good luck
   b) see what more I can get
   c) make my boss happy

158

3) When Keith didn't **make the grade** as a professional athlete, he decided to become a high school football coach instead.
   a) succeed
   b) fail
   c) get good grades

4) Kim is interested in working internationally, and she hopes to get a job in Europe **down the road**.
   a) after she retires
   b) close to home
   c) in the future

5) Sure, Michelle earns more money than any of us and has the biggest office, but **she's earned her keep**.
   a) she earns a lot of money
   b) she just got lucky
   c) she deserves it

6) **I'm not sure how to break the news**, but our company is bankrupt and our offices will close down next week.
   a) I've got some wonderful news to tell you
   b) This is difficult to discuss
   c) I'm not sure whether or not this is true

7) Nordstrom's department stores are famous for their customer service. They're always willing to **go the extra mile** to please their customers.
   a) travel long distances
   b) do a lot
   c) do nothing

8) Melissa didn't get the job offer at the *Los Angeles Times*. They told her they needed somebody with more journalism experience **who could hit the ground running**.
   a) who would run away from the job after a short period
   b) who could tell everybody else how to do their jobs
   c) who would learn quickly how to do the job

ANSWERS TO LESSON 26, p. 204

You didn't lift a finger on that project.

FIRING SOMEBODY
炒某人魷魚

Kurt has the difficult task of firing Dan. Dan's been with the company since the beginning and is a friend of Kurt's. Dan is surprised and upset with the news.

Kurt: Dan, **your work has slipped**. You've been here for 15 years, and I think you're just **burned out**.

Dan: What are you talking about? I'm **at the top of my game**. I just managed our biggest project in years.

Kurt: You can't **take credit for** that. You **didn't lift a finger** on that project. You were on vacation in Hawaii for three weeks while Steve and Sally were doing all the work.

Dan: I'm not good at **reading between the lines**. Please just **cut to the chase**. What are you trying to say?

Kurt: Dan, Swift Shoes is *downsizing*. This is really difficult, but we're going to have to **let you go**.

Dan: What? I helped **build this company from the ground up**! You can't fire me now.

Kurt: I don't want to, but **my hands are tied**. Our president has told me to **reduce headcount** by 50 percent.

Dan: I thought you and I were friends, but **when push comes to shove**, I guess our friendship isn't worth anything.

Kurt: Of course we're still friends, but business is business.

Dan: I don't agree with that. I would never fire a friend…after all those times Kathleen and I invited you and Donna to dinner at our home!

Kurt: Dan, I want you to leave Swift Shoes on friendly terms. **No hard feelings**. To **soften the blow**, we're going to give you a generous *severance package*.

IDIOMS & EXPRESSIONS - LESSON 27

one's work has slipped　工作表現下滑
one's performance has gotten worse; one is not doing one's job properly

EXAMPLE: What's going on with Jeremy? He used to be very good at his job, but recently **his work has slipped**.

....

(to be) burned out　筋疲力竭
to be extremely tired; to lose effectiveness because of doing a job for too long

EXAMPLE: After working 80-hour weeks at the investment bank for many years, Jim was **burned out**.

....

(to be) at the top of one's game　（工作表現）正值顛峰狀態
to be performing at the top of one's abilities; to be performing very well

EXAMPLE: Last year, Ethan brought in over $5 million in new business to the agency. He's **at the top of his game**.

....

(to) take credit for something　搶功
to claim recognition for something

EXAMPLE: Joan came up with the idea of selling the company's products at Costco, but her boss **took the credit for it**.

(to) not lift a finger 完全沒幫到忙
to not help at all; to do nothing

EXAMPLE: While everybody else was working hard to finish the project, Tim was chatting with his friend and **didn't lift a finger**.

(to) read between the lines 解讀弦外之音
to understand unclear or indirect communication; to interpret something from hints or suggestions

EXAMPLE: Your boss told you to take a very long vacation? **Read between the lines**: he's suggesting you leave the company!

ORIGIN: This expression comes from the days when people would send secret messages. When treated with a special substance like lemon juice, a secret message would appear between the lines of an ordinary looking letter. Therefore, when told to "read between the lines," you should look for the hidden meaning.

(to) cut to the chase 開門見山
to get to the point; to tell the most important part of the story

EXAMPLE: I don't have time to listen to a long explanation of why you didn't finish this project on time. Please **cut to the chase**.

ORIGIN: In action films, the "chase" refers to most exciting part, when the drama is at a high point. Some people may want the movie to get to this exciting part (in other words, cut to it) as soon as possible.

(to) let someone go 炒某人魷魚
to fire someone

EXAMPLE: Mepstein Industries **let their accountant go** after he made a major mistake calculating the company's tax bill.

(to) build something from the ground up 從草創期開始幫助／建立根基
to develop a company, a business, or a department from its beginnings; to build a successful operation from scratch

EXAMPLE: Autumn Moon Vineyards doesn't yet have a marketing department. They're going to have to **build one from the ground up**.

my hands are tied 我也沒辦法
there's nothing I can do; I'm stuck; I have no alternatives

EXAMPLE: I don't approve of the direction my company is moving in, but my boss doesn't want to listen to my opinion. **My hands are tied**.

(to) reduce headcount 裁員
to lay off or fire workers

EXAMPLE: When Lucent's business was in trouble, they announced they would **reduce headcount** by at least 10,000 employees.

NOTE: "Headcount" is the number of people who work at an organization. Many companies do not like to say that they are "laying people off" as it can sound cold and insensitive. After all, *people* are involved. "Reducing headcount" gets around this problem. It sounds less personal and more scientific.

SYNONYM: to downsize

when push comes to shove 面臨考驗時／緊要關頭
when really tested; when it really counts; when there's no more time left to hesitate or think about what action to take

EXAMPLE: Many people say they are worried about the environment, but **when push comes to shove**, how many people are willing to pay extra for environmentally-friendly products?

SYNONYM: when you come right down to it

no hard feelings 別介意／沒生氣
no anger; no bitterness

EXAMPLE: Even though Hewlett-Packard didn't give Derek a job offer, he has **no hard feelings** towards them.

(to) soften the blow 降低傷害
to try to lessen the damage or pain

EXAMPLE: While it's never pretty, there are things you can do to **soften the blow** of bad news.

❧ PRACTICE THE IDIOMS

Fill in the blanks, using the following idioms.

> no hard feelings
> work has really slipped
> at the top of her game
> burned out
> reduce headcount
> let them go
> her hands are tied
> build the company from the ground up

Liz is in a difficult position. Her boss has told her to _____(1)_____ since the company is in financial trouble. Liz only has three employees: Brian, Rachel, and Pam. Brian and Rachel are doing great work, so she can't afford to _____(2)_____ . Pam isn't doing so well. In fact, over the past year her _____(3)_____ . It's true that Pam helped _____(4)_____ and has been a very loyal employee over the past 10 years. Unfortunately, she's no longer _____(5)_____ . Liz thinks Pam has simply worked too hard and is now _____(6)_____ . Liz likes Pam, and would prefer not to fire her. But _____(7)_____ . Liz hopes there will be _____(8)_____ after she tells Pam the bad news.

ANSWERS TO LESSON 27, p. 204

In my last job, I wore many hats.

JOB INTERVIEW 1
面試（一）

Donna, a Human Resources Manager, is interviewing Marina for a sales position.

Donna: Tell me about your most recent work experience.

Marina: Right now I'm **between jobs**. In my last position, I was a marketing associate at Comtek International. I was there for two and a half years.

Donna: I know I've heard of them, but I'm **drawing a blank** right now. What do they do?

Marina: They produced international trade fairs. They were **bought out** last month by a much larger company and all of us were **let go**.

Donna: I see from your résumé that you also worked in sales for the company.

Marina: Yes, that's right. It was a small company, so **I wore many hats**. It was very exciting.

Donna: What are you looking for in a job?

Marina: Well, I'm a real **people person**, so I would like to take a position where I have lots of *interaction* with different people.

Donna: Describe your ideal boss.

Marina: I work well with all different types of people. But I guess my ideal boss would be **hands-off**. I prefer to work independently and not to be **micro-managed.**

Donna: Tell me about a time when you had to **think outside the box** in your work.

Marina: When I was at Comtek, we didn't have any money to buy advertising. I **put in place** a program offering magazines a stand at the trade show in exchange for an advertisement in the magazine.

Donna: That sounds like a good idea! Tell me, what **sparked your interest** in our sales position?

Marina: I noticed from your job description that it requires a lot of interaction with the marketing department. I'm very interested in marketing, so I thought this would be a good **stepping stone** to a marketing position.

Donna: Yes, this would be a good way to **get your foot in the door** of the marketing department.

IDIOMS & EXPRESSIONS - LESSON 28

between jobs 待業中
out of work; unemployed

EXAMPLE: Barbara is **between jobs** right now. She hopes to find a new job soon.

NOTE: Saying one is "between jobs" sounds better than saying one is "unemployed."

(to) draw a blank 記不得
to be unable to remember

EXAMPLE: I can't remember the name of the hotel where we stayed in Budapest. I'm **drawing a blank**.

(to) buy out 收購
to purchase an entire business or someone's share of the business

EXAMPLE: When Victor's company was **bought out** by Microsoft, he was able to retire.

(to) let someone go
see Lesson 27

(to) wear many hats 身兼數職
to perform many different job responsibilities; to play many different roles

EXAMPLE: There are only five employees at our company, so we all have to **wear many hats**.

people person 樂群之人
somebody who likes working with people; a friendly person

EXAMPLE: You're sure to like Paul. He's a real **people person**.

hands-off 別插手干涉太多
not too involved; passive; not interested in managing details

EXAMPLE: Don't worry, Chris won't get involved in all of your projects. He's a **hands-off** manager.

(to) micro-manage 事事介入
to manage too closely; to be too involved in the details

EXAMPLE: Heidi gets involved in every detail of her employees' work. She has a reputation for **micro-managing**.

(to) think outside the box
see Lesson 6

(to) put in place 建立／執行
to establish; to start; to implement

EXAMPLE: Next month, the company plans to **put in place** some new rules for filing expense reports.

(to) spark one's interest 引起某人的興趣

to raise one's interest; to cause one to become interested in

EXAMPLE: An article in the *Wall Street Journal* **sparked Don's interest** in investing in Brazil.

stepping stone 踏腳石

a way of advancing or getting to the next stage; a position, a product, or an activity that comes first and prepares the way for what will come next

EXAMPLE: Jennifer views her position as a human resource manager as a **stepping stone** to a larger position within her company.

(to) get one's foot in the door 帶某人入門／跨出第一步

to get into an organization; to take a position with an organization that could lead to a bigger opportunity in the future

EXAMPLE: Taking a job as a receptionist is one way to **get your foot in the door** of a company.

✎ PRACTICE THE IDIOMS

Choose the best substitute for the phrase or sentence in bold:

1) We received résumés from two candidates that **sparked our interest**. Please call them to arrange interviews.
   a) will definitely be hired
   b) aren't interesting
   c) look promising

2) I'm currently **between jobs**, but I'm confident I'll find something soon.
   a) on vacation
   b) employed
   c) unemployed

3) No wonder Carl is so good at sales. **He's a real people person.**
   a) He's good with people.
   b) He's good at his job.
   c) He doesn't like people.

4) Working at a small company with only four employees, Vijay is used to **wearing many hats**.
   a) working much too hard
   b) putting on a hat every morning
   c) doing many different things at work

5) Working as a summer intern is a good way to **get your foot in the door with a company**.
   a) get a full-time job at a company
   b) get promoted
   c) make money over the summer

6) Where does Wendy work? I know she told me, but **I'm drawing a blank**.
   a) I wasn't listening
   b) I can't remember
   c) I promised not to tell anybody

7) I suggest you take the sales analyst position. It's a **stepping stone to a better position.**
   a) way to get a better job in the future
   b) way to ensure you'll always be a sales analyst
   c) way to guarantee you'll be the sales director next year

8) Angela hardly ever sees her boss. **He's hands-off.**
   a) He keeps his hands off her.
   b) He doesn't manage her closely.
   c) He has his hands in everything.

ANSWERS TO LESSON 28, p. 204

I snapped up these chairs for a song.

JOB INTERVIEW 2
面試(二)

Sam currently runs his own company selling used office furniture online. He's tired of running his own business and wants to get a job with a big company.

Nick: I see from your résumé that you're **running your own show** as the owner of OldOfficeChair.com.

Sam: That's right. I've **carved out a niche** selling used office chairs over the Internet.

Nick: That sounds like a great business.

Sam: I was **making money hand over fist** after the *dot-com bust*. Companies were **going belly up** every day, and I **snapped up** all their chairs **for a song**. But these days it's becoming harder and harder to find used chairs.

Nick: Wouldn't you rather continue working for yourself?

Sam: No, I'm tired of working for myself.

Nick: I can **see the writing on the wall**: you'll **jump ship** when you think up another good business idea.

Sam: No, I won't. I'd always wanted to be an entrepreneur, but I **got that out of my system**. I realize now that **it's not all it's cracked up to be**.

Nick: It certainly isn't. You work really hard and you're just as likely to **strike out** as you are to **strike it rich**.

Sam: **Tell me about it!** My best friend invested all his money in starting a company. He ended up **losing his shirt!**

Nick: Right, we all know people like that...One final point about the position. As you know, this is a large corporation. Are you sure you wouldn't be happier at a **start-up**?

Sam: **Start-ups** are exciting, but at this point in my life, I'm looking for stability over excitement. I've got four kids at home, and they like to eat!

Nick: I hear what you're saying. We could use somebody around here who thinks like an entrepreneur. If you're someone who can **take the ball and run with it**, you'd be a great addition.

IDIOMS & EXPRESSIONS - LESSON 29

(to) run one's own show 獨當一面／全權掌控經營
to run one's own business; to have control over an entire business or a part of a business

EXAMPLE: Anne can't imagine working for somebody else. She loves **running her own show** as CEO of Anne Global, Inc.

....

(to) carve out a niche 另闢一個市場／另闢蹊徑
to start a specialty business

EXAMPLE: Teresa **carved out a niche** selling DVDs on eBay.

NOTE: A "niche" is the market segment served by a particular product, service, or product line.

....

(to) make money hand over fist 大賺一筆
to make a lot of money; to make a lot of money fast

EXAMPLE: AstraZeneca **made money hand over fist** with the drug Prilosec. It was a huge success.

174

(to) go belly up 破產
to go bankrupt

EXAMPLE: Shortly after Borders bookstore opened downtown, the small bookshop **went belly up**.

(to) snap up 大量購進
to buy for a very good price; to buy a large supply of something, usually because it's on sale or in short supply

EXAMPLE: While in Vietnam, Monica **snapped up** dozens of inexpensive, beautiful silk scarves to sell at her Manhattan clothing boutique.

for a song 很便宜
cheaply, inexpensively

EXAMPLE: Monica was able to buy jewelry and clothing in Hanoi **for a song**.

(to) see the writing on the wall 預見將來會發生的事
to know what's coming; to see what's going to happen in the future

EXAMPLE: The company has canceled this year's holiday party. I can **see the writing on the wall**: soon, they'll be announcing lay-offs.

NOTE: You will also see the variation: handwriting on the wall.

(to) jump ship 離職
to quit a job; to leave a job suddenly

EXAMPLE: When the accounting scandal broke, several financial managers at the energy company **jumped ship** immediately.

(to) get something out of one's system 覺得做某件事已經做夠了，不需要再……
to no longer feel the need to do something; to experience something to one's satisfaction

EXAMPLE: Tom had always wanted to be a lawyer, but after his summer internship at a law firm, he **got that out of his system**.

175

not all it's cracked up to be　沒大家想的那麼偉大
not as great as people think; not as great as its reputation

EXAMPLE: Working for a big public relations firm is **not all it's cracked up to be**. The pay isn't great and the hours are long.

(to) strike out　失敗
to fail

EXAMPLE: I'm sorry to hear that you **struck out** on the job interview. I'm sure something else will come along soon.

(to) strike it rich　一夜致富
to attain sudden financial success; to get rich quickly

EXAMPLE: Victor **struck it rich** when Microsoft bought out his small software company.

Tell me about it!　我完全同意
I agree with you

EXAMPLE: "Our CEO really needs to get some new suits." — "**Tell me about it!** His suits are all at least 25 years old!"

(to) lose one's shirt　輸得一文不剩
to lose everything one owns; to lose a lot of money in business; to make a very bad investment

EXAMPLE: It's risky to invest all of your money in the stock market. If the market goes down a lot, you could **lose your shirt**.

start-up　新成立的小公司
a small business, usually one that's been operating five years or less (and often in the technology industry)

EXAMPLE: Julie took a chance by leaving her secure job at IBM to join a risky **start-up**.

(to) take the ball and run with it　主動出擊╱不需上司交代
to take initiative; to take charge without a lot of supervision

EXAMPLE: We told the graphic designer what to include in the brochure, and she was able to **take the ball and run with it**.

176

❧ PRACTICE THE IDIOMS

Choose the most appropriate response to each sentence:

1) We purchased an entire office building in New York for a song a few years ago when the economy was bad.
   a) Now that building would be much more expensive.
   b) Now that building would be much cheaper.
   c) Now you could probably get that building at a good price.

2) Carol, our new finance manager, is the type of person who can take the ball and run with it.
   a) Great, we need somebody here who needs a lot of direction.
   b) Great, we need some more good athletes in our office.
   c) Great, we're looking for somebody with initiative.

3) Jesse won $5 million last month in a lawsuit. He really struck it rich.
   a) No wonder he's decided to retire!
   b) No wonder he's decided to go to law school!
   c) No wonder he's decided to continue working!

4) We're looking to hire somebody who'll stay with our company for at least a few years. You wouldn't jump ship after just a year, would you?
   a) No, I don't even like sailing.
   b) No, I always stay at jobs at least three years.
   c) No, I would probably quit after a year.

5) You might get rich investing in biotech companies, but you're just as likely to lose your shirt.
   a) That's good advice. I'll definitely invest heavily in them.
   b) That's true. I'd better be careful about putting too much money into them.
   c) That's true, but I'd be willing to give away my shirt in exchange for a lot of money.

6) While in Russia, you should snap up some lacquer boxes. They're beautiful and inexpensive there.
   a) Okay, I will be sure to pack plenty of boxes.
   b) Okay, I will be sure to sell some lacquer boxes.
   c) Okay, I will be sure to buy some lacquer boxes.

7) I bought plane tickets on Econo-Airlines, and a few days later they went belly up!
   a) I'm sure you'll have a great flight.
   b) I'll be sure to book my next flight with Econo-Airlines.
   c) That's too bad. You'd better buy some new plane tickets.

8) Working on Wall Street for an investment bank sounds wonderful, but it's not all it's cracked up to be.
   a) You're right. It really is wonderful.
   b) You're right. The pay is good, but the work is demanding and the hours are long.
   c) You're right. Everybody I know who works on Wall Street loves it.

ANSWERS TO LESSON 29, p. 204

NEGOTIATING A SALARY OFFER
Part 1
談薪水

Donna calls Marina to tell her the good news — she got the job. Marina wisely decides to negotiate for a higher salary.

Donna: Marina, it's Donna Harris from American Steel Enterprises. I've got great news. We'd like to make you an offer.

Marina: That's fantastic!

Donna: Our HR department will go over the **nitty-gritty** of the offer with you, but let me give you **the big picture** now. The *base salary* will be $45,000.

Marina: I'm really excited about this opportunity. I should mention that I'm **weighing another offer** with a higher *base salary*. **Is there any room to negotiate**?

Donna: What did you **have in mind**?

Marina: Well, my other offer is for $50,000. Can you match it?

Donna: That's **out of our range**. Let's **split the difference**. We'll go up to $47,500.

Marina: Can we say $48,000?

Donna: No, I'm afraid not. Our final offer is $47,500.

179

Marina: This sounds good, but I'd like to **sleep on it**. Can I call you back tomorrow?

Donna: Yes, but please **touch base with** me **first thing in the morning** so we can **get the ball rolling**. We've got several other candidates interested in the position.

Part 2: The Next Day

Marina: Donna, I've had a chance to **review your offer**. I'm going to **stand my ground**. To accept your offer, I really need $48,000.

Donna: Marina, you **drive a hard bargain**! But, okay, I think that can be arranged. Can you start on Monday, 9 a.m.?

Marina: That'll be perfect. See you then!

IDIOMS & EXPRESSIONS - LESSON 30

nitty-gritty   細節
the details

EXAMPLE: I don't need to know the **nitty-gritty** of what happened during your meeting with the client. Just tell me the main points.

NOTE: The exact origins of this are unknown. This expression belongs to a class of fun expressions with sounds that repeat themselves. Other such expressions include: wishy-washy (see Lesson 8), itsy-bitsy (very small), fuddy-duddy (a boring, old-fashioned person), and mish-mash (a strange combination of things).

the big picture   大前提／重點
a summary; an overview; the most important points

EXAMPLE: Let me start off this presentation by giving you **the big picture** of what's happening now in our industry.

(to) weigh another offer 考慮另一個工作
to consider another offer, usually a job offer

EXAMPLE: Brian told Pfizer he was **weighing another offer** and that he would give them an answer next week.

Is there any room to negotiate? 提有議價的空間嗎？
Is it possible to negotiate? Are you flexible about the offer?

EXAMPLE: Your offer is a little lower than I had hoped for. **Is there any room to negotiate?**

(to) have in mind 心裡所想的
to be thinking of

EXAMPLE: Kyle said he wanted to go somewhere exotic for this year's company offsite. Do you know where he **had in mind**?

out of one's range 超過上限
more than one wants to pay

EXAMPLE: PlastiCase Industries tried to sell us the cases for five dollars each, but we told them that was **out of our range**.

(to) split the difference 折衷
to accept a figure halfway in between; to compromise

EXAMPLE: You're asking for $500 for this used office chair, but we only budgeted $300 for it. Let's **split the difference** and say $400.

(to) sleep on it 考慮一天看看
to think about a decision overnight; to take a day to decide on something

EXAMPLE: Thanks for your offer, but I'm not sure I want to move from the marketing department to the sales department. Let me **sleep on it**.

(to) touch base with – see Lesson 3

first thing in the morning 一大早
early in the morning

EXAMPLE: If the report isn't ready by the time you leave this evening, please have it on my desk **first thing in the morning**.

(to) get the ball rolling 開始
to get started

EXAMPLE: If the toy company wants to have their new line of mini-robots out by the holiday season, they'd better **get the ball rolling** now.

(to) review an offer 考慮所提的條件
to think about an offer; to consider an offer

EXAMPLE: After **reviewing your offer** carefully, I've decided to take a job with another company.

(to) stand one's ground 堅持立場
to maintain and defend one's position; to refuse to give up one's position

EXAMPLE: Earthy Foods wanted to open a large grocery store in the historic downtown area, but the small town **stood its ground** and refused to let them build there.

(to) drive a hard bargain 談判太高竿
to be tough in negotiating an agreement; to negotiate something in one's favor

EXAMPLE: We don't usually offer such a big discount on our products, but you **drove a hard bargain**.

🖎 PRACTICE THE IDIOMS

Fill in the blanks, using the following idioms.

> first thing in the morning   drive a hard bargain
> split the difference   weighing another offer
> room to negotiate   out of our range
> big picture   review our offer

Karen: Hi, it's Karen Chen from Citigroup calling to see if you've had a chance to _____(1)_____ .

Rick: Hi, Karen. I still haven't made up my mind. I'm _____(2)_____ from another financial services company.

Karen: Oh really? What are they offering? Just tell me the _____(3)_____ . I don't need to know the details.

Rick: They're offering a base salary of $80,000, plus bonus.

Karen: Oh, goodness. I'm afraid $80,000 is _____(4)_____ .

Rick: Well, I'm still very interested in Citigroup. Is there any _____(5)_____ ?

Karen: Our offer to you was for $65,000. We can _____(6)_____ and offer you $72,000.

Rick: Your offer would be more attractive at $75,000 with a guaranteed bonus of $7,500.

Karen: You _____(7)_____ ! Let me talk to our senior management. I'll get back to you tomorrow, _____(8)_____ .

ANSWERS TO LESSON 30, p. 204

REVIEW FOR LESSONS 26-30

Fill in the blank with the missing word:

1) We've discussed this issue long enough. Let's just cut _____ the chase and make a decision.

    a) at   b) up   c) to

2) If you want to get your _____ in the door of an advertising agency, you should try to get an internship.

    a) body   b) foot   c) leg

3) This past quarter you sold over \$1 million worth of insurance policies. Keep _____ the good work!

    a) at   b) with   c) up

4) Companies are making money hand _____ fist selling music downloads over the Internet.

    a) over   b) above   c) upon

5) Right now Rachel doesn't want to take an international assignment. However, she might consider working in China down the _____.

    a) lane   b) street   c) road

6) Emily was sure that her analysis was correct, so she stood her _____ when others criticized it.

    a) field   b) opinion   c) ground

7) You're selling color photo printers for only \$39? People are sure to snap those _____!

    a) down   b) through   c) up

8) Judy gets bored doing the same thing all day. She's looking for a job where she's required to _____ many hats.

   a) wear   b) sew   c) make

9) Dale decided to retire after General Mills bought _____ his small organic food company.

   a) up   b) out   c) in

10) Debra took a job as program assistant with a non-profit organization, hoping it would be a stepping _____ to a management position in the future.

   a) point   b) stone   c) rock

11) You don't have to give Frank a lot of detailed direction. He knows how to take the ball and _____ with it.

   a) run   b) walk   c) jump

12) We'd be interested in renting this office space from you if you can lower the price. Four thousand dollars per month is simply _____ our range.

   a) within   b) into   c) out of

13) Martin was laid off from his job six months ago, and he still hasn't found a new position. He's _____ jobs.

   a) among   b) between   c) out of

14) These days, you can register domain names on the Internet _____ a song.

   a) in   b) for   c) with

15) If you're having trouble reaching a decision, why don't you sleep _____ it and give your answer tomorrow.

   a) with   b) over   c) on

ANSWERS TO REVIEW, p. 204

bells and whistles the name of the game track record the best of both
worlds on top of trends through the roof on the same page nothing is set
in stone put a st⋯⋯ a nutshell noth-
ing to sneeze at a p⋯ up to the plate dream
up on the right track generate lots of buzz more bank for the buck wear

GLOSSARY OF TERMS

ad campaign　宣傳活動
short for **advertising campaign**. The creation of a series of advertisements placed in
various media (such as radio, TV, Internet) designed to promote a particular product
or product line.

agenda item　議程事項（議項）
one thing on a list of things to be discussed at a meeting

analytical　邏輯的分析
relating to analysis and the ability to solve problems in a logical manner

(to) associate a brand with　將品牌聯想到⋯⋯
to link a company's brand in one's mind to something positive; to make the connection between a brand and something else

base salary　基本工資
the salary not including bonuses or any other benefits

brand equity　品牌價值
the value that a company's brand name adds to the product or service; the mix of all
parts that go into making up the brand: quality, awareness, loyalty, emotion

CFO　財務長
short for **chief financial officer**. The senior manager responsible for the financial
activities of a company.

company offsite　辦公室外的員工（休閒、訓練）活動
a trip in which employees of a company leave the office together and go to another
location, frequently for fun or to discuss broad company goals for the future

corner office 角落辦公室（指專為企業合夥人、執行長、高階主管保留的辦公室）
the most prestigious office location in a company, generally reserved for senior management

differentiated products 市場區隔產品
products with distinct features or characteristics that distinguish them from the competition

dot-com bust 網路泡沫化
the period from 2000-2002 when many Internet companies went out of business

(to) double-check （仔細檢查）複核／查
to verify; to check something again

(to) downsize 縮編／精簡人事
to reduce the number of employees; to dismiss from work

endorsement 代言／背書
a promotional statement; a signal of approval

ergonomic 符合人體工學（的產品）
products designed to fit the shape of the human body, usually very comfortable and easy to use

figure 財務數字
an amount of money (in number form, for example $4500)

focus group 焦點團體（市場調查者用來了解商品或議題所選出最具代表性的一群人）
a type of market research in which a small group is gathered and asked their opinion about a product or idea. Focus groups are often used to evaluate new product ideas or new advertising campaigns.

forecast 市場預測
an estimate of the future demand for a product or service

franchise 連鎖店／授權加盟機構
an independent business which sells the products or services of a larger company. The independent business is called the "franchisee," while the larger company is called the "franchisor." The franchisee typically pays a fee to the franchisor in the beginning and then pays a percentage of all sales.

freebie 贈品
a free thing; something that is given away for free, usually as part of a promotional campaign

fruit smoothie 水果冰沙
a drink made in a blender, consisting of fruit juice, whole fruit, ice, and sometimes yogurt

grand 一千（美元）　　　thousand

innovative 創新
being or making something completely new; original

interaction 互動
acting together with others; working closely with others

inventory 盤存／存貨
finished and unfinished products which have not yet been sold, plus raw material (parts to be put together)

(to) launch 開發／開始／啟動
this word has several definitions, but in this situation, the meaning is: to introduce to the market; other definitions include: 1) to start or initiate (to launch a new career); 2) to set in motion (to launch a rocket)

(to) launch a website 架設網站
to put a new website on the Internet

low carb 低碳水化合物
short for **low carbohydrate**. Refers to a diet which is low in carbohydrates. Low-carb diets gained popularity in 2002, made popular by nutrition expert Dr. Atkins. Many food and beverage companies produced low-carb diet foods to make money on the popularity of the diet.

market demand 市場需求
the total demand for products or services

mascot 吉祥物
an animal or person used as a symbolic figure by an organization, typically a company or a sports team

optional 非必須的
not required; possible but not necessary

overtime pay 加班費
money paid to an employee for hours worked above the number of hours he or she is required to work

overview 摘要　　a summary

P & L 盈虧
short for **profit & loss**. Those with P&L responsibility are in charge of making sure the business makes a profit. They manage the "P & L statement," also called the "income statement." This statement shows the results of financial operations over a certain time period, usually a month, a quarter, or a year.

perks （額外）津貼
short for **perquisites**: benefits other than salary

price quote 報價／估價　　an estimate

private-label products 自有品牌產品
products manufactured by one company and branded and marketed under a different company name; a cheaper alternative to a national brand (very often a store brand); a product manufactured and labeled especially for a certain store and only sold at that store

product life cycles 產品生命周期
the stages a product goes through starting with its introduction. These stages are typically: introduction, growth, maturity, decline. The marketing strategy is based on where a product is in its life cycle.

product line 產品線
a group of similar products; a group of related products that are marketed together by the same manufacturer

pros and cons 優缺點
advantages and disadvantages

prototype 原型
an original model of a new product, usually used to evaluate the design and production process before the finished product is manufactured

R&D 研發
short for **research & development**. The R&D department at a company is responsible for coming up with new and improved products and processes and often for testing products to ensure a certain level of quality is reached or maintained.

rag 品質粗糙的小報
this word has several definitions. Here, the meaning is: a low-quality newspaper filled with advertisements and poorly-written articles.

reference 推薦函
a recommendation by a past employer to a future employer regarding a person's character and qualifications

relic 古董／古物
outdated and obsolete; *literally:* an object that has survived the passage of time; an object of religious worship, such as the finger of a saint

salary freeze 凍結加薪
a temporary stop to pay raises due to a company's financial problems

severance package 遣散費／資遣安排
the benefits offered to an employee being laid off

sexual harassment 性騷擾
unwelcome verbal or physical contact of a sexual nature that affects one's employment or creates an unpleasant work environment

shopping cart （購物網站上的）購物車
in the technology world, an electronic order form used by shoppers online to select and buy merchandise; the software that enables electronic commerce transations

short by 短缺
under by; still missing some product

strip joint　脫衣舞酒吧

a bar in which women remove their clothes on stage for the entertainment of male clientele (during "ladies' night" male performers take their clothes off for the entertainment of female clientele)

summer intern　暑期實習生

a student serving an apprenticeship at a company over the summer to gain experience in a particular field

tough　艱難　　difficult

Please visit our web-site, where you'll find:

- Additional practice exercises for **Speak Business English Like an American**
- Interesting links for studying English
- More books from Language Success Press

www.languagesuccesspress.com

LESSON 1: TALKING ABOUT A NEW PROJECT

1. b
2. a
3. b
4. a

5. c
6. c
7. a
8. b

LESSON 2: TALKING ABOUT FINANCIAL ISSUES

1. a
2. b
3. c
4. b

5. a
6. a
7. c
8. b

LESSON 3: DISCUSSING A NEW AD CAMPAIGN

1. b
2. a
3. a
4. b

5. c
6. a
7. c
8. b

LESSON 4: TALKING ABOUT MANUFACTURING

1. 24/7
2. does whatever it takes
3. work out the kinks
4. fine-tuning

5. working down to the wire
6. cutting it close
7. reality check
8. get the job done

LESSON 5: TALKING ABOUT COMPANY STRATEGY

1. b
2. c
3. b
4. b

5. a
6. b
7. c
8. c

REVIEW: LESSONS 1-5

1. b	4. c	7. c	10. b	13. c
2. a	5. c	8. b	11. c	14. b
3. a	6. a	9. a	12. b	15. a

LESSON 6: DISCUSSING GOOD RESULTS

1. b	5. c
2. c	6. a
3. a	7. b
4. a	8. b

LESSON 7: DISCUSSING BAD RESULTS

1. running in place
2. eating their lunch
3. no wonder
4. on top of trends
5. bring some new products to market
6. in deep trouble
7. face the music
8. new blood

LESSON 8: DISCUSSING A DIFFICULT DECISION

1. b	5. c
2. c	6. b
3. b	7. a
4. a	8. b

LESSON 9: DEALING WITH A DISSATISFIED CUSTOMER

1. deliver
2. Where to begin
3. a far cry from
4. mince words
5. pulled out all the stops
6. pull the wool over my eyes
7. pretty penny
8. make it up to you

LESSON 10: DISCUSSING A DIFFICULT REQUEST

1. c	5. c
2. a	6. b
3. a	7. a
4. b	8. c

REVIEW: LESSONS 6-10

1. b	4. a	7. a	10. a	13. b
2. c	5. c	8. c	11. b	14. c
3. c	6. b	9. a	12. b	15. b

LESSON 11: MOTIVATING CO-WORKERS

1. turn around our business
2. throw in the towel
3. count me in
4. on board
5. rally the troops
6. team spirit
7. working their tails off
8. track record

LESSON 12: RUNNING A MEETING

1. b	5. a
2. c	6. c
3. b	7. c
4. a	8. b

LESSON 13: DISCUSSING A MISTAKE

1. I could've sworn that
2. drop the ball
3. asleep at the wheel
4. blow things out of proportion
5. no big deal
6. dot your i's and cross your t's
7. up to scratch
8. bitter pill to swallow

LESSON 14: TAKING CREDIT FOR GOOD RESULTS

1. a	5. b
2. b	6. a
3. c	7. a
4. b	8. c

LESSON 15: SHIFTING BLAME

1. c	5. c
2. b	6. a
3. b	7. c
4. a	8. a

Review: Lessons 11-15

1. c	4. a	7. b	10. c	13. a
2. b	5. c	8. a	11. a	14. c
3. c	6. b	9. a	12. b	15. c

Lesson 16: Politely Disagreeing with Someone

1. c	5. a
2. a	6. c
3. b	7. a
4. b	8. c

Lesson 17: Telling Somebody Off

1. pulling his weight	6. slave driver
2. sick and tired	7. run a tight ship
3. the last straw	8. turn a blind eye
4. shape up or ship out	9. cut me some slack
5. What's the deal?	10. spare me the sob story

Lesson 18: Discussing Office Scandals

1. c	5. b
2. b	6. b
3. a	7. a
4. b	8. c

Lesson 19: Complaining about a Co-worker

1. hot-head	5. grin and bear it
2. steer clear	6. in a snit
3. issues with her	7. get bent out of shape
4. gets under his skin	8. push my buttons

Lesson 20: Talking about a Brown Noser

1. a	5. b
2. c	6. a
3. c	7. c
4. b	8. b

REVIEW: LESSONS 16-20

1. b	4. c	7. a	10. b	13. c
2. a	5. b	8. c	11. a	14. b
3. c	6. b	9. a	12. c	15. b

LESSON 21: EXPLAINING THAT YOU'RE FEELING OVERWORKED

1. a	5. c
2. c	6. b
3. b	7. b
4. a	8. a

LESSON 22: CALLING IN SICK

1. under the weather	5. I'm not feeling so hot
2. killing me	6. there's something going around
3. call in sick	7. take it easy
4. up to my ears in work	8. in tip-top shape

LESSON 23: REQUESTING A BANK LOAN

1. b	5. c
2. a	6. a
3. b	7. c
4. b	8. c

LESSON 24: NEGOTIATING A PURCHASE

1. more bang for the buck	5. no can do
2. break my budget	6. nickel-and-dime
3. the hard sell	7. on a tight budget
4. at no extra charge	8. it's a deal

LESSON 25: CONDUCTING A PERFORMANCE REVIEW

1. b	5. c
2. b	6. a
3. c	7. a
4. a	8. b

Review: Lessons 21-25

1. c	4. a	7. c	10. c	13. b
2. b	5. b	8. b	11. a	14. a
3. b	6. a	9. b	12. c	15. b

Lesson 26: Promoting an Employee

1. c	5. c
2. b	6. b
3. a	7. b
4. c	8. c

Lesson 27: Firing Somebody

1. reduce headcount
2. let them go
3. work has really slipped
4. build the company from the ground up
5. at the top of her game
6. burned out
7. her hands are tied
8. no hard feelings

Lesson 28: Job Interview 1

1. c	5. a
2. c	6. b
3. a	7. a
4. c	8. b

Lesson 29: Job Interview 2

1. a	5. b
2. c	6. c
3. a	7. c
4. b	8. b

Lesson 30: Negotiating a Salary Offer

1. review our offer
2. weighing another offer
3. big picture
4. out of our range
5. room to negotiate
6. split the difference
7. drive a hard bargain
8. first thing in the morning

Review: Lessons 26-30

1. c	4. a	7. c	10. b	13. b
2. b	5. c	8. a	11. a	14. b
3. c	6. c	9. b	12. c	15. c

Speak English Like an American

說一□道地生活美語

written by AMY GILLETT

LEARN THE IDIOMS & EXPRESSIONS YOU NEED TO SUCCEED ON THE JOB!

WHAT'S THE SECRET TO SPEAKING ENGLISH FLUENTLY?

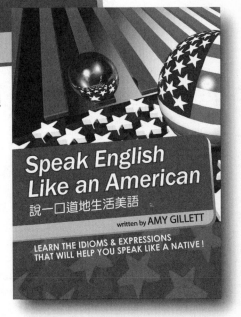

Speak English Like an American

說一□道地生活美語

written by AMY GILLETT

LEARN THE IDIOMS & EXPRESSIONS THAT WILL HELP YOU SPEAK LIKE A NATIVE!

If you already speak English, and you'd like to start speaking even better, then *Speak English Like an American* is for you. Thousands of people in the United States and around the world have already improved their English using Speak English Like an American. Now it's your turn!

In this deluxe book & CD set, you'll find:
- ★ Over 300 of today's most common American English idioms & phrases
- ★ Several usage examples of each idiom
- ★ Dozens of exercises to reinforce the material—complete with answer key so you can correct yourself
- ★ Crossword puzzles to practice your new expressions
- ★ 25 lively dialogues—the entertaining story of an American family, complete with illustrations